HISTORY FAIR

The true story of Hunter Scott
and the USS Indianapolis

A screenplay by
Jeanne (JT) Larson
Writing as
Jeannie Depp

Second edition

ISBN-13:
978-0692679371 (Aykeen Press)
ISBN-10:
0692679375

Printed in the United States of America

We've all seen it, that scene in Jaws where Robert Shaw as Quint tells the story of how the USS Indianapolis sank, giving gritty and emotional detail to the horrors the survivors faced in those cold, unforgiving waters. What we didn't all know is that it was true. It really happened.

That in itself, is more of a horror story than the movie that made it famous. That shark, at least, was fake. The ones that took those men were terribly real.

And, to add insult to injury, the men that came out of the water were subjected to outright lies about what happened and who was responsible for it. They were left with nothing but the memories of those days when they were left for dead, adrift in the open sea.

The truth did come out, decades later, thanks to the determination of a boy who saw something that was wrong and wanted to set it right. He took on the Navy and became the youngest person to ever testify before a Senate Arms Committee to set the record straight and overturn a court martial that should never have happened.

Survivors were on hand to see it, and I'm glad. They deserved to have their dignity restored and to be recognized with the respect they've earned.
I saw a quick snippet about Hunter in 2003 and contacted the Scott family. With their

kind permission and cooperation, I wrote
a script about Hunter and his involvement
with the USS Indianapolis and her
survivors.

It's hard, writing about real people and
events that happened in their lives. The
Scott family, as well as the brave men that
served aboard the doomed USS Indianapolis,
and the ones who died when she went down,
they are remarkable people who deserve to
be well represented. Theirs is a story that
I felt then, and still feel today, deserves
to be told and told well.
I hope I've done that.

As of this writing, there are currently two
movies in the works about the USS
Indianapolis. One, starring Nicolas Cage
is due out this year (2016). The second is
the (as of yet untitled) Hunter Scott
Project. Still in the early stages of
pre-production, the only real information
available right now is that Robert Downey
Jr is slated to co-produce.

Beck when I first wrote the script, the
Scott family gave it to the (then)
potential producer. It was considered
along with two other scripts. But it was
all very casual. There was nothing
official going on. Nobody's heard much
about it since then. I sure haven't.
The project has changed hands a great many
times since then. Nobody really knows
what's up with it. The only thing that's
certain is that they rights to the movie

were optioned (bought) by Warner Brothers in 2011. That's when Robert Downey Jr's name came up.

Since then, the Scott family hasn't really been involved. They know about it, but no real specifics. The only thing Hunter has had to say about it in the press is that he hopes the film does those brave men justice.

So do I.

When I wrote the script, I gave it the title History Fair for two reasons. First, because one of the early stages of Hunter's journey involved a project that he put together for a history fair to raise awareness about the Indy and her crew. Secondly, that's what he did. He made history fair. He set it right.

I hope that my words can a part of telling this story on film. But even if they aren't, I maintain the highest optimism for this story, and for the movie that results. It is, simply, a good story. I wish it the very best of luck.

Jeannie Depp

INT. THE senate arms committee - DAY

We begin with an empty, black screen.
We can't see anything yet, but we can
HEAR the noises that happen in a large
room with a lot of people in it who are
trying to be quiet but not succeeding.
The shifting of feet on the floor,
backsides shifting on wooden seats,
and hushed whispers. The kinds of
sounds you might hear in a courtroom.

Over the low din, a quiet voice speaks
through a microphone.

                    HUNTER
               (VO)
          My name is Hunter Scott.

All the other sounds in the room hush
completely.

                              FADE UP TO:

INT. THE SENATE ARMS COMMITTEE - DAY

Fourteen year old Hunter Scott is a
well-groomed teenage boy, with a tidy
haircut and a responsible suit. The
very picture of a clean-cut
all-American boy.

Hunter looks small sitting at a heavy
wooden table, holding a piece of paper
in both hands, from which he is
reading.

                    HUNTER
          I am a ninth grade student
          from Pensacola, Florida.

Even with the microphone, Hunter's
voice is hard to hear.

From off-screen, we HEAR Chairman
Warner speak.

                  CHAIRMAN WARNER
          We are going to ask you to
          raise your voice a little
          bit, and draw the microphone
          up-

Hunter looks up at the person who
spoke, composed but a little
startled.

From a WIDER ANGLE, we see that Hunter
is sitting in front of a panel of men
wearing heavily decorated formal
military dress uniforms. Chairman
Warner, the man who spoke, is in the
center of the panel.

Behind Hunter is a gallery that looks
like a who's who of the naval military
community, ranging from enlisted men
to seasoned veterans with enough
brass on their chests to build a
battleship.

Toward the back of the room, the media jockey for position with cameras and tape-recorders, listening intently.

Seated directly behind Hunter, in the front row of the gallery, are several older men, some in wheelchairs, wearing caps with a picture of a battleship embroidered on the front, decorated with VFW pins.

                    HUNTER
          Yes sir.

                    CHAIRMAN WARNER
          Somewhat closer.

                    HUNTER
          Yes sir. I'm sorry.

                    MR. MURPHY
          Pick it up and push it toward
          you, if you can.

SENATOR SMITH reaches over to help Hunter move the microphone closer so the committee can hear him better.

                    CHAIRMAN WARNER
          Yes. Speak right into it.

Hunter gathers himself without missing a single beat and continues.

                    HUNTER
          My journey to this committee
          as a witness began over
          three years ago when I
          watched the motion picture
          "jaws" with my father.

EXT. OUTSIDE THE SCOTT HOUSE

The exterior of the Scott house
appears to be the typical Florida
home, drenched with sunshine with
tropical plants landscaped in the
yard.

                         TITLE OVER:
                 Summer 1996
             Pensacola, Florida

INT. THE SCOTT HOUSE

11 year-old Hunter walks into the
living room where his dad is sitting
on the sofa. ALAN SCOTT has the remote
control in his hands, ready to watch
a movie.

Hunter flops dramatically onto the
other end of the couch.

                    ALAN
          What's the matter, son?

                    HUNTER
          It's too hot to do anything.

                    ALAN
          Do you want to sit down and
          watch this with me?

                    HUNTER
                    (warily)
          What is it?

                    ALAN
          My favorite movie.

          Hunter and Alan say unanimously:

                    HUNTER AND ALAN
             Jaws!

          Both of them laugh.

                    HUNTER
                    (playfully)
          Again? (He smiles) Yeah,
          okay.

          Hunter settles onto the floor and
          watches the movie, propped up on his
          elbows, his chin propped in his hands

          We HEAR the familiar sounds of the
          movie "Jaws", including the telltale
          MUSIC and the SOUNDS of the sea.

          Hunter and Alan both react to the
          movie, grimacing and looking
          frightened at all the right spots.

Then a scene starts that causes them
both to lean forward, held rapt by the
speech.

Scene from the movie "Jaws":

Quint, Hooper and Brody are in the
cabin of the ORCA. It's at night, it's
dark, and the three men are trapped in
the cabin of that boat surrounded by
the night sea and the monster shark
out there in it. To pretend they
aren't all thinking of what's waiting
for them in the sea, the men are
drinking and laughing over tales of
battle scars.

Brody points at a scar on Quint's arm.

> BRODY
> What's that one?

> QUINT
> What?

> BRODY
> That one there. On your arm.

> QUINT
> Oh. That's a tattoo. I got
> that removed.

> HOOPER
> Don't tell me. (He giggles)
> Don't tell me. Mother.

Carried away by the jovial mood and
quite amused with himself, Hooper
breaks down into fits of laughter.

Quint's not laughing anymore.

>   QUINT
>   No, Mister Hooper. That's
>   the USS Indianapolis.

Hooper sobers instantly. He regards
quint with sober awe and incredulity.

>   HOOPER
>   You were on the
>   Indianapolis?

>   BRODY
>   (Good-naturedly,
>   unaware that the
>   mood has taken a
>   somber turn)
>   What happened?

Quint looks up at Brody and begins to
tell it. The entire time, Hooper sits,
stunned, and listens. He's studied
these things, but that's not the same
as hearing it from somebody who was
there and survived it.

>   QUINT
>   Japanese sub. Slammed two
>   torpedoes into our side,
>   chief.
>   (MORE)

We was comin' back from the
island of Tinian Delady.
Just delivered the bomb. The
Hiroshima bomb.

Quint pauses for a second, gearing up
to tell the horrible story of what
happened.

                QUINT (CONT'D)
        Didn't see the first shark
        for about half an hour.
        Tiger. Thirteen-footer. You
        know how you know that when
        you're in the water, chief?
        You can tell by looking from
        the dorsal to the tail. What
        we didn't know was that our
        bomb mission had been so
        secret, no distress signal
        had been sent.

Quint takes another drink.

Brody looks at Quint soberly,
realizing fully that this is no longer
a laughing matter.

                QUINT (CONT'D)
        They didn't even list us
        overdue for a week. The very
        first light, chief, the
        sharks come cruisin'. So we
        formed ourselves into tight
        groups.
                (MORE)

Sort of like old squares
that you see in a calendar,
the battle of Waterloo, and
the idea was the shark comes
to the nearest man and he'd
start pounding and
hollering and screaming.
Sometimes the shark would go
away. Sometimes he wouldn't
go away.

Quint looks into the distance as he
tells it. Robert Shaw does a fine job
of looking like a man who's lived
through a nightmare and is having to
relive it in the telling.

                    QUINT (CONT'D)
Sometimes that shark he
looks right into you, right
into your eyes. You know a
thing about a shark, he's
got lifeless eyes. Black
eyes like a doll's eyes.
When he comes at you he
doesn't seem to be livin'.
Until he bites you, and
those black eyes roll over
white and… Oh then you hear
that terrible high-pitched
screaming and the ocean
turns red. In spite of all
the hollering and pounding
they all come in and rip you
to pieces.
                    (MORE)

You know, by the end of that first dawn we lost a hundred men. I don't know how many sharks, maybe a thousand. I don't know how many men. They averaged six an hour. Oh Thursday morning, Chief, I bumped into a friend of mine. Herbie Robinson from Cleveland. Baseball player. Boson's mate. I thought he was asleep. I reached over to wake him up. He bobbed up and down in the water, like a kind of top. Upended. Well, he'd been bitten in half below the waist. Noon the fifth day, Mister Hooper, a Lockheed Ventura saw us, he swung in low and he saw us. He was a young pilot, a lot younger than Mister hooper. Anyway, he saw us and he come in low, and three hours later, a big fat PBY comes down and starts to pick us up. You know, that was the time I was most frightened, waiting for my turn. I'll never put on a life jacket again. So. Eleven hundred men went into the water, three hundred and sixteen men come out. The sharks took the rest, June the twenty-ninth, nineteen forty-five.

Quint's voice cracks on the last word,
his throat heavy and dry from telling
a tale that had been caught in it for
a long time.

Quint pauses, and drags himself back
to the present with dark sarcasm.

                    QUINT (CONT'D)
          Anyway, we delivered the
          bomb.

Quint takes another drink. Hooper and
Brody stare at him in stunned silence.

INT - THE SCOTT LIVING ROOM.

The SOUNDS of the movie on the
television continue, including the
trademark music, oceanic slapping of
the water against the hull and the
occasional SREECHING of a gull.

                    HUNTER
                  (VO)
          "Jaws" is my dad's favorite
          movie, so I've probably seen
          it a hundred times. But I
          think that was the first
          time I really listened to
          that part about the
          Indianapolis. I mean, that
          couldn't really have
          happened, could it?
          Something that horrible?

Like the men in the movie, Hunter and Alan sit in silence at the end of Quint's speech. On their faces is the same stunned expression. The sheer impact of that speech is not lost on these two.

Hinter sits up and looks at his father over his shoulder.

                    HUNTER (CONT'D)
          Dad, is that true?

                    ALAN
          Yes, and please move from in
          front of the TV.

                    HUNTER
          That really happened? Will
          you tell me more about it?

Alan cranes his neck to look around Hunter, who has not moved from in front of the television.

                    ALAN
          I'll tell you what. I have to
          do some research for my
          dissertation, so I'll take
          you to the library with me
          and you can look it up for
          yourself. How about that?

                    HUNTER
          Okay, Dad. Thanks.

Hunter settles back down to watch the rest of the movie. We HEAR all the gruesome details.

INT - THE LIBRARY

Alan sits Hunter down at a table with a stack of books, paper, and a pencil.

                ALAN
        Start with these. Use the
        index, go through these and
        write summaries of
        everything you find out
        about the USS Indianapolis.

                HUNTER
        Okay Dad. Maybe we could go
        fishing later?

Alan smiles warmly at his son.

                ALAN
        Maybe, son. I'm going
        upstairs to the stacks. I'll
        be back in an hour.

Alan leaves Hunter to his research.

Hunter buckles down to it. He traces along the list of subjects in the first book, looks closer, and flips through the book. He reads for a moment and starts to write on the pad.

Upstairs in the library, Alan looks over the railing to where Hunter sits reading. He smiles at how hard his son is working.

Hunter slides off the chair and approaches the librarian at the desk.

                    HUNTER
          Ma'am, can you please help
          me find some other books
          about Word War II?
          Especially the USS
          Indianapolis?

                    LIBRARIAN
          Certainly. Let me see what I
          can find.

                    HUNTER
          Thank you.

Hunter goes back to his seat.

The librarian taps on her computer's keyboard, looks at the screen and writes down some information.

The librarian places a few more books on the table beside Hunter's other books. Hunter smiles and thanks her politely, then picks up one of the new books.

With all the books opened in front of him, Hunter looks at his legal pad.

There are only a few lines written there. Perplexed, he sits back.

Alan returns.

                    ALAN
          Let's see what you've got.

Alan looks at Hunter's notes.

                    ALAN (CONT'D)
          There's not much here. What
          have you been doing for an
          hour?

                    HUNTER
          I've been reading, Dad.
          Honest. There just isn't
          very much in these books
          about the USS Indianapolis.

                    HUNTER (CONT'D)
                    (VO)
          Dad gave me that look. He
          doesn't want to call me a
          liar, but something like
          this HAS to have more
          written about it. Right?

Alan looks at Hunter skeptically and
pulls a book closer to him.

                    ALAN
          Let's have a look together
          and see if we can't find some
          more information, shall we?

Alan looks through the books. Like
Hunter, he doesn't find much
information at all. He pulls another
book closer and looks through it, too.
And then another.

                    ALAN (CONT'D)
          There has to be something
          wrong. This has to be the
          worst naval disaster in
          history. How can there not
          be more thoroughly
          discussed in the history
          books? There's got to be
          more to it than this.

                    HUNTER
               (VO)
          But there wasn't. I looked
          in every book I could find,
          and there just wasn't
          anything more. Why not?

Alan thinks a moment.

                    ALAN
          Let's try something else.

INT - THE MICROFICHE SECTION

Alan and Hunter huddle close in front
of the microfilm reading machine.
Alan is working the controls, and
they're both trying to read.

Headlines and images from 1945 float quickly across the screen, ghosts from the past. One headline mentions the sinking of the Indianapolis, and the Captain of the Indianapolis, Charles B. McVay.

Hunter lingers on this screen, reading it carefully.

                    HUNTER
          They blamed the Captain? But
          a Japanese SUB sank the
          ship. That doesn't make any
          sense.

                    ALAN
          That's what it says.

                    HUNTER
          Could we make copies of
          these?

                    ALAN
          Sure. We can print them.

Pages file on top of each other out of the printer, and Alan gathers them up into a neat stack. He shows Hunter how to put them carefully into their own manila folder.

Hunter takes the folder.

As Hunter rand Alan pass the counter on their way out of the library, one

librarian approaches Hunter with a
book.

                    LIBRARIAN
          Young man, here's another
          book you might try.

Hunter takes the book and smiles.

                    HUNTER
          Thank you ma'am.

Hunter turns the book over in his
hands. It's called "Fatal Voyage."

                    HUNTER (CONT'D)
          Dad, can we check this one
          out?

                    ALAN
          Sure, son.

INT - HUNTER'S BEDROOM - NIGHT

Hunter's mom finishes tucking Hunter
into bed and leaves the room, turning
off the light and closing the door.

Hunter watches her leave. When he's
sure she isn't coming back, Hunter
takes a flashlight out from under his
pillow and begins to read under the
sheet with the flashlight.

OUTSIDE HUNTER'S DOOR

Hunter's mother has paused here, and sees the darting light of Hunter's flashlight under the door, smiles and leaves. She could very easily go back in and take away the book, but she allows him to read.

                    TITLE OVER:

July 29, 1945

THE USS INDIANAPOLIS - DAYTIME

The bow of the Indianapolis slices cleanly through the water of the blue and silver sea.

On her deck, seamen go about their business, many with their shirts off. The bright daylight reflects off all the clean surfaces, including the dog tags that hang on chains around the men's necks and lay glistening against their chests.

                SEAMAN 1
     I'll tell you what, boys. I
     don't know what that cargo
     was we let off at Tinian, but
     I'm glad it's gone.

                    SEAMAN 2
          I know what you mean,
          brother. That has bad news
          written all over it. I'm
          glad to see it go.

Another seaman comes through with his
tools in hand. He pushes his way
good-naturedly between the two.

                    SEAMAN 3
          That's yesterday's news,
          buys. You know what
          tomorrow's news is, don't
          you?

                    SEAMAN 1
          No, smartass. What's
          tomorrow's news?

                    SEAMAN 3
          The Philippines! Think
          about it! Filipino girls!
          How fun in the sun!

                    SEAMAN 2
          You need to cool off, man. We
          ain't even there yet and you
          got your jets all in an
          uproar. It's just not
          healthy, I tell ya!

                    SEAMAN 3
          Me, I'm sleeping topside
          tonight. It ain't likely to
          cool me off, though, if you
          know what I mean.

Seaman 3 winks to convey his meaning.

                    SEAMAN 3 (CONT'D)
          Life is good, boys.

                    SEAMAN 1
          Sleeping topside? You don't
          get in trouble for that?

                    SEAMAN 2
          Hot as it is? Nah. They don't
          care as long as they don't
          trip over you. Gotta beat
          this head SOME kind of way.

SEAMAN 1 hitches his thumb in the
direction of seaman 3

                    SEAMAN 1
          Yeah, especially him.

                    SEAMAN 2
          There's only one cure for
          the hots he's got, mister.
          And I'm not volunteering for
          it.

The men laugh heartily.

Over the shoulder of the crewmen, in
the distance, the captain of the
Indianapolis, Charles B. McVay,
ascends the stairs to the command
deck. He's dressed in his short
sleeves, has a cup in one hand and a
binder under his arm.

He hears his men laughing, and pauses.
Good-natured fun undermines military
efficiency not in the least, and is
good for the men. Especially men in
wartime. He smiles with them and
continues upstairs.

INT - PENSACOLA JUNIOR HIGH SCHOOL
CAFETERIA

Hunter takes "Fatal Voyage" out of his
book bag. He eats his lunch with one
hand and holds his place in the book
open with the other as he intently
reads some more.

INT - USS INDIANAPOLIS COMMAND DECK

                CREWMAN 1
      Attention! Captain on deck!

Everyone on the command deck snaps to
attention.

McVay responds quickly, standing only
briefly on ceremony.

                         MCVAY
              As you were.

The men relax their posture and return
efficiently to their duties.

McVay takes his place, putting down
his cup and binder. He reviews the
notes of the shift on the clipboard.
It's routine, business as usual.

                    MCVAY (CONT'D)
              Helmsman, route Peddie to
              Leyt, please. Make your
              speed seventeen knots.

                       HELMSMAN
              Aye, sire. Peddie to Leyt.
              Seventeen knots.

                       FLOYD
              No escort, sir?

                       MCVAY
              They denied us an escort.
              But all the action is north
              of us, so we should be fine.

The captain looks out the window at
the sky.

                    MCVAY (CONT'D)
              Looks about right. I want to
              make chop by Monday.

THE CAPTAIN SPEAKS TO THE HELMSMAN

> MCVAY
> Discontinue zig-zag. Let's
> get there.

> HELMSMAN
> Aye, sir. Discontinue
> zig-zag.

INT - HUNTER'S ROOM - NIGHT

Hunter sits on his bed, in a small pool
of light from his flashlight,
reading.

THE INDY - NIGHT

In the deep night of the Pacific, the
Indianapolis sleeps. She is barely a
silhouette in the moonlight.

TITLE OVER:

Sunday night, July 29, 1845

ON THE DECK

In the clear moonlight, a sailor
stretches out on the deck to sleep. He
puts his shoes under his head for a
pillow. There are a few other sailors
laid out on the deck to sleep, too. The
sea rocks a lullaby and the men sleep
soundly.

IN ONE OF THE TURRETS

A sailor is relieved by his replacement. The relieved sailor lights a cigarette as he leaves his post.

BELOW DECK - SLEEPING BAYS

Sailors slumber deeply on bunks in a dark sleeping Bay. The quietest disturbed only by a random snore or the shift of the bodies we know fill this sleeping Bay.

ON THE BRIDGE

The clock reads that it's just after midnight.

IN HIS CABIN

Captain McVay sleeps, laying on top of the sheets and blanket on his bunk.

THE ENGINE ROOM

In the huge, cavernous engine room, even the sounds of the machines seem subdued in deference to the night. The mechanical noises are rhythmic, the steadily beating heart of the sleeping ship.

                    HUNTER
               (VO)

     They were all asleep. How
     could they know it was going
     to happen?

EXT - UNDERWATER - THE HULL

Only the slightest hints of light
reach the hull under the water,
especially at night. A few glimmers of
light glide along the smooth skin of
the ship.

The calm is shattered when two
torpedoes tear gaping holes in the
ship's hull.

INT - THE ENGINE ROOM

Water roars rushing into the engine
room through the ruined hull with
relentless force.

The flood of water slams into the
machines there, making them scream
and stop working. Steam hisses up from
them and is washed away.

Men scurry up the wire staircases for
the door, but don't make it. They are
washed out of sight by the relentless
flood pouring into the ship.

INT - CAPTAIN MCVAY'S CABIN

The captain is thrown to the floor by
the impact. Smoke fills the room
period he recovers quickly, gets up
and runs out his door.

INT - THE PASSAGEWAY

Men run for their lives, yelling. We
HEAR one shouting something about
explosions, and another about
sinking.

The alarms are blaring and the
emergency lights blink on.

EXT - THE DECK

The sleeping men on deck are jolted
awake by the explosion. The deck lists
behind them, and several are thrown
over the side.

INT - THE SLEEPING BAY

Men caught below scream in the chaos.
The whole world lists to the side.
Men, the bunks, and every other object
in the Bay are thrown around by the
violent lurching of the ship.

INT - THE BRIDGE

McVay runs in and the bridge crew
members quickly give captain McVay
status reports when he bursts in.

                    ORR
          I've lost all communication.
          I've tried to stop the
          engines, but I don't know if
          the order got through.

                    MCVAY
          Send word down to Radio 1 to
          get out a distress message.
          Fast!

                    ORR
          If I can, sir.

                    MOORE
          Sir, forward compartment
          flooding fast. We're badly
          damaged and taking on water.
          Do you want to abandon ship?

                    MCVAY
          Maybe we can hold her. I
          don't want any more men to
          die who don't have to. Is
          there any word from the
          radio room?

                    ORR
          No Sir. Nothing.

INT - THE RADIO ROOM

Radio tech MINER is thrown out of his
chair. Chief tech WOODS hold his seat.
Miner struggles to get back up,
glancing from the radio console to the
door. Miner looks to woods for what he
should do. Woods orders him out.

                    WOODS
          You need to get out of here.
          Go get a life jacket on! Go!

Miner goes.

INT - THE BRIDGE

                    FLYNN
          We've been badly damaged,
          Charlie. We're taking water
          fast. The bow is down. I
          think we're done for. I
          recommend we abandon ship.

                    MCVAY
          Commander Flynn, pass the
          word to abandon ship. Nobody
          goes over the side without a
          life jacket! Get the floater
          nets against the stack.

                    FLYNN
          Sir?

                    MCVAY
          You heard me! All hands
          abandoned ship!

Orr rushes out.

INT - BELOW DECKS PASSAGEWAY

Men rush past Orr with towels on their
heads struggling to get topside. They
are panicked, running for their
lives. Meanwhile, Orr tries to get
below.

INT - THE RADIO ROOM

In contrast to the smoking, dark
passageway, Orr finds the emergency
lights working in the radio room.
Seated at the counsel, tech Woods
looks up at Lieutenant Orr. Orr can
see that woods has been burned, but is
still working, nonetheless.

                    ORR
          We have to get a distress
          message out right by God
          now!

                    WOODS
          I'm way ahead of you, Sir.

Woods gets up from his station and
hands Lieutenant Orr a copy of the
message he's just sent.

It reads:

USS INDIANAPOLIS… TORPEDOED TWICE…
LATITUDE TWELVE DEGREES NORTH,
LONGITUDE ONE HUNDRED THIRTY FIVE
DEGREES EAST… NEED IMMEDIATE
ASSISTANCE…

The ship shudders, jerks, and lists
violently.

                    ORR
        Out, now! We're abandoning
        ship! Get out!

They both rush out.

EXT - TOPSIDE

More men are jumping into the ocean.
The entire ship is rapidly becoming
engulfed in flames and smoke.

The screams of the men, the horrible
tearing sound of metal and the roar of
rushing sea are cut short by a change
of shots too:

INT - HUNTER'S BEDROOM

The book hits the floor.

Hunter looks down at the book, then
across the room at the portrait of
captain McVay that sits in the central
place of honor on his dresser. The

portrait seems to look at Hunter,
trying to connect with him through the
barrier of the years that have gone
by.

                HUNTER
     But it wasn't your fault.

EXT - THE OPEN SEA

Beneath the surface of the Pacific,
the Indianapolis sinks. There are no
more screams, now. It's silent.
Slowly, the last hint of Gray metal
fades out of view.

INT - THE SCOTT LIVING ROOM - DAY

Hunter approaches his dad. He has an
envelope in his hand.

                ALAN
     What have you got there?

                HUNTER
     It's a letter to the
     president, asking him if he
     will change the record. It
     wasn't captain McVay's
     fault that his ship sank.
     Can I please have a stamp?

Alan gives Hunter a look.

                ALAN
     Say that again?

                    HUNTER
          May I please have a stamp?

Alan smiles at Hunter's dedication.
It's sweet and brave of Hunter to try.

                    ALAN
          I'll mail it for you, if you
          like.

                    HUNTER
          Thanks, dad.

                    HUNTER (CONT'D)
               (VO)
          He did mail it for me, too.
          A few weeks later, I even got
          a letter back. Beat it said
          "No."

INT - PENSACOLA GRADE SCHOOL - HUNTER'S
CLASS - DAY

The classroom is empty except for
Hunter and his teacher, Mrs.
PREVATTE. She's seated at her desk,
looking at the papers Hunter has
brought to show her. They include the
printouts from the microfiche, the
pictures of McVay and the
Indianapolis, and also Hunters
handwritten notes.

Hunter stands beside the desk
politely waiting for the teacher to

finish looking at everything. She
does, and looks at him.

                    MRS. PREVATTE
          This looks fascinating. I
          think it would make a very
          interesting project.

Hunter smiles.

                    HUNTER
          Thanks. I thought it would.
          The only problem is that's
          all the information I can
          find. That's all there is.
          Anywhere.

The teacher carefully stacks the
papers back into Hunter's folder and
hands it to him.

                    MRS. PREVATTE
          Do you think any of these men
          might still be alive? The
          survivors of an incident can
          often be the best source of
          information about it.

Hunter brightens at the suggestion.

                    HUNTER
          That's a great idea. Thanks!

Hunter grabs up his notes and rushes
out.

INT - THE SCOTT KITCHEN

Hunter is seated at the kitchen table. In front of him on the table are printouts from the Internet and a phone book. He's got the phone book open and is tracing his finger up and down the tiny typewritten rows of names and numbers.

Mrs. Scott enters the kitchen and sees her son with his face buried in the phone book.

                    MRS. SCOTT
          Honey? What are you doing?

                    HUNTER
          I'm trying to find some of
          the survivors from the
          Indianapolis.

                    MRS. SCOTT
          Why don't you try putting an
          ad in the paper? Pensacola
          is a pretty big Navy town.
          You might get an answer from
          somebody who can help you.

                    HUNTER
          That's a great idea! What do
          you think it should say?

                    MRS. SCOTT
          What are you trying to do?

                    HUNTER
          If I can talk to some of the
          survivors, maybe they can
          tell me what really happened
          so I can put it in my history
          fair project.

                    MRS. SCOTT
          That sounds like a pretty
          good place to start, son.
          Introduce yourself and say
          what it is you hope to
          accomplish.

Hunter smiles at the new idea. He
pushes the phone book away, picks up
his pencil and starts to write on his
paper.

INT - NEWSPAPER CLASSIFIED OFFICE

Hunter hands the clerk a piece of
paper and pays for the add. Behind
Hunter, Alan watches. This is
Hunter's business and Alan let him do
it himself without interfering.

INT - THE GROCERY STORE

Alan picks up a newspaper from the
rack and opens it.

INSIDE we see Hunters ad. It reads:

USS INDIANAPOLIS
Looking for survivors of the
USS Indianapolis to interview
for my History Fair Project.
Contact Hunter Scott at (850)
555-2690.

INT - BELL'S LIVING ROOM

MAURICE GLEN BELL receives a copy of
the paper. He opens it and sees the ad.

He puts down the newspaper, takes off
his reading glasses and covers his
eyes with an unsteady hand.

He is an older man with thinning hair
age spots on the backs of his hands,
and a haunted look on his face. He's
just read something that wiped away
more than 50 years' worth of his
defenses against that past that he's
built for himself. He could have come
out of the water yesterday.

Beside Mr. Bell there is a picture of
the young sailor he used to be,
Standing proudly in front of the
Indianapolis, smiling and innocent
before surviving her sinking.

Mr. Bell takes his hand away from his
eyes and gathers himself.

Mr. bell, when he is able, puts his hand on the phone and picks it up.

INT - THE SCOTT HOME

Mr. Scott picks up the phone.

                ALAN
     Hello?

He pauses, listening.

                ALAN (CONT'D)
     Yes Sir, Mr. Bell. It is. I'm
     Hunter's father. Yes, of
     course. I'll get him.

INT - HUNTER'S ROOM

Alan opens the door and comes into the room. Hunter is sitting on the floor surrounded by all of his papers and research.

                ALAN
     Hunter, there's a phone call
     for you.

Hunter looks up, curious.

INT - THE SCOTT LIVING ROOM

Hunter picks up the phone.

                HUNTER
     Hello?

Hunter listens for a moment.

                    HUNTER (CONT'D)
               (VO)
          The man on the phone was Mr.
          Maurice Glen Bell. He had
          survived the sinking. When
          Mr. Bell invited us to meet
          him, my dad never even
          hesitated.

INT - MR. BELL'S HOUSE

Hunter is sitting on the floor in
front of Mr. bell, who is seated in his
comfortable old leather recliner.

Hunter turns Mr. Bell's Purple Heart
medal over in his hands and examines
it.

                    HUNTER
          What do they put on it to
          make it purple?

Mr. Bell smiles warmly down at Hunter.

                    BELL
          I'm not quite certain.

Hunter looks at Mr. Bell with obvious
respect and begins to ask questions
with a frankness that is neither rude
nor intrusive. Finding out is why he
came here, and telling it is why Mr.
Bell let him.

                    HUNTER
How long were you on board
the Indianapolis?

                    BELL
Two years, before she went
down.

                    HUNTER
Do you remember what you
were doing when the
torpedoes hit?

                    BELL
I was asleep. I thought a
boiler had exploded. That's
what I thought.

Echoes from the distant past, we hear
the explosions and whispers of the
chaos that followed the impact of the
torpedoes.

While Hunter sits and politely
listens, Mr. Bell continues to talk.

                    HUNTER
                 (VO)
He told me the story of how
the Indianapolis sank, just
like he remembered it. He
told me all of it.

INT - THE SLEEPING BAY

Bell, as the young man he was in 1945,
tumbles from his bunk in the sweeping
Bay. He joins the chaos headed for the
Hatch and goes topside.

EXT - ON THE DECK

Bell sees a life jacket on the deck and
bends to take it but someone else
snatches it away. He spies another
one, grabs it, and puts it on while he
makes his way to the side of the ship.

Bell sees other men jumping off the
side of the ship, one of them stark
naked, and he jumps off, too.

EXT - IN THE WATER

Bell swims as hard as he can to get
away from the ship.

                    HUNTER
                  (VO)
        When a ships sinks, it will
        create a Whirlpool that can
        suck you down with But, if
        you don't get far enough
        away. Mr. Bell got far
        enough away from it, though.
        A lot of them did.

From the water, Giles McCoy looks back
and watches the ship sink.

Other men ump from the sides of the
ship, and some jump from the fantail
at the back. McCoy screams helplessly
for them to stop but there's no way for
them to hear him, and probably no
chance that they would listen anyway.

ON THE FANTAIL

A man jumps off the fantail. It's his
only option, with the boat on fire and
going down fast.

From the POV of the falling man we see
the propellers rushing up to meet us,
huge, turning, and lethal.

EXT - IN THE WATER

McCoy raises his hands in a gesture to
suggest he would catch the falling,
doomed men if he could. It's a
helpless, horrified gesture

EXT - ELSEWHERE IN THE WATER

A man who isn't wearing a life jacket
grabs onto Bell and his attention is
diverted from the ship. He holds the
other man up the best he can.

At different distance intervals, we can HEAR the screams and choking of other men who had jumped off the boat.

From a distance, we see the flaming bulk of the Indianapolis slip beneath the water.

INT - HUNTER'S BEDROOM DESK

Hunter's sitting at his desk, stuffing Manila envelopes and licking them shut.

                    HUNTER
                (VO)
        Mr. Bell gave me the names of
        more survivors. To prepare
        for the history fair, I sent
        out questionnaires to the
        remaining survivors.

INT - THE POST OFFICE - DAY

Alan approaches the counter with a yellow card in his hand. He hands it over to the cashier.

                    ALAN
        Hi. This says there was too
        much mail for my box? Is that
        right? Thanks.

The postal worker takes the card, departs, and returns quickly with a large bundle of mail. Each letter in

it is addressed to Hunter. Many bear
stamps or stickers representing the
Navy.

                HUNTER
            (VO)
        There were one hundred and
        fifty-four survivors left.
        They all wrote me back.

INT - HUNTER'S BEDROOM

Hunter sits cross-legged on his
bedroom floor, surrounded by the
letters from the survivors. He's
reading them one by one.

                HUNTER
        Some of them said they never
        told anybody before. But
        they told me. They told me
        everything. Just like Mr.
        Bell did. I know they were
        doing it to help me, but I
        think it helped them too.

EXT - THE OPEN SEA - DAYTIME

Bell clings to a large floating net,
along with a large group of men. Since
he has on a life jacket and isn't hurt,
he's still in the water. Other men who
don't have on jackets, or who do show
signs of injury or on top of the net.

                    HUNTER
                (VO)
    Since the ship kept moving
    forward after it started to
    sink, not all of the men were
    together. Some of the groups
    were miles apart. There were
    some on the nets, and some in
    rafts. Some didn't have
    anything at all to hold them
    up.

ELSEWHERE ON THE OPEN SEA

There are men with captain McVay and
a small group of rafts tied together.
They have a few tins of food.

AT THE NETS

Bell sees a man who had drifted twenty
feet away from the nets. Bell calls
out to him, when the man screams. A
shark takes him down quickly and he
never comes back up. Horrified, Bell
clings up the Nets.

                    HUNTER
                (VO)
    By the second day, sharks
    were everywhere. They took
    men whenever they wanted,
    and no yelling or splashing
    ever made them go away. It
    wasn't like in a movie at
    all.

ON THE RAFTS

There are four or five rafts lashed
together. The men in one of them begin
to untie their raft from the others.

                    BLUM
          We're going to paddle to
          yap. It's only a couple 100
          miles.

The others try to stop them.

                    REDMAYNE
          That's crazy! You won't make
          it! Come back!

The renegade raft floats out of sight,
the men in it paddling for all they're
worth.

                    HUNTER
                (VO)
          They left anyway. A few days
          later, they were all dead.

AT THE NETS

One man puts his face down in the
water. Bell grabs him and tries to
hold him up but the man gives up and
dies anyway.

Bell takes the man's dog tags and then
lets him go. The man slips silently
beneath the water.

Bell puts the tags into the net.

                    SAILOR ON THE NETS
          Hey, are you stealing from
          that guy? Do you have some
          food?

                    BELL
          No food. I'm just taking his
          dog tags for his family.

                    HUNTER
               (VO)
          Hunger and thirst do bad
          things to a man's body. It
          can do worse things to a
          man's mind. A lot of the men
          hallucinated that they
          could see islands or food or
          girls. Some of the men
          ducked under the surface and
          drank salt water, really
          believing it was fresh from
          the Indy's galley. Some did
          worse.

EXT - THE OPEN SEA - NIGHT

In the dark of night, one seaman,
presumably dead, lays half in the
Nets, half in the water. There is a
gash in his throat leaking blood.
Another sailor licks his lips with a
thick tongue and leans toward the
wound with his mouth open hungrily.

COZELL SMITH turns away, horrified.

                    HUNTER
               (VO)
          That could have been a
          hallucination and not real
          at all. Either way, Cozell
          said the image was burned
          into his mind and he will
          never be able to forget it.

INT - THE SCOTT HOUSE - NIGHT

Hunter lowers the letter after he
finishes reading it, looking a little
horrified himself.

                    HUNTER
               (VO)
          Neither will I.

Hunter puts the letter aside, rather
than including it with a stack of
letters he's already read.

EXT - THE OCEAN - DAYTIME

On the nets, in the rafts or floating
freely in the water, men cover their
eyes and tie shirts around their heads
for cover from the sun. It's the only
thing they can do, except wait.

                    HUNTER
                (VO)
"It's scary," one of them
said. "Especially when a
shark swims between your
legs." I don't think I could
stand five minutes of
that, not knowing when a
shark could grab you and
drag you under. I don't know
how they survived five days
like that.

                         TITLE OVER:

AUGUST 3RD, 1945

INT - INSIDE THE LOCKHEED VENTURA

Pilot Lieutenant WILBUR C. GWINN is
flying his plane on a routine patrol
over the ocean. The day is bright, the
sky is clear.

An indicator light catches Gwinn's
attention.

                    GWINN
Damn it. It looks like the
antenna wire got loose
again.

                    COPILOT
Didn't we just get that
fixed?

                    GWINN
          Here. You fly the bird. I'll
          go take a look. It should
          only take me a second to slap
          it around a little.

He winks at his copilot.

                    GWINN (CONT'D)
          She likes it rough.

In the rear of the plane, GWINN and his
machinist mate lean out the hatch and
see the antenna whipping around
wildly. Below them, out the Hatch, the
men see bright glistening ocean as
well as the rebellious antenna.

                    GWINN (CONT'D)
          All right. Let's reel the
          damned thing in and tie a
          piece of rubber hose on the
          end of it. That should hold
          it until we get back in.

A patch of the ocean below the Hatch
turns ugly and black.

                    MACHINIST MATE
          Look. Oil slick. There must
          be a sub down there.

                    GWINN
          Wait a second. there are
          bumps in it… Those are men!
          All the way out here in the
          middle of nowhere? Drop a
          life raft, some clean water,
          and a sonobuoy.

The ordered items fly out of the back
of the plane and land in the water near
a group of men who start to shout and
wave.

                    MACHINIST MATE
          Do you think they're
          Japanese?

                    GWINN
          No, look. There's more of
          them. There's got to be more
          than a hundred and fifty.
          Japanese Subs don't carry
          that many. These have to be
          Americans.

                    MACHINIST MATE
          Where the hell did they come
          from? Way out here?

                    GWINN
          Who cares! Drop everything
          we've got for them! My God,
          get on the radio! Now!

INT - HUNTER'S BEDROOM - DAY

Hunter puts down the last letter.

> HUNTER
> (VO)
> Then it was over. The men
> that were left got picked
> up. Hearing all of it was
> even more chilling than
> jaws. It was real.

INT - HUNTER'S BEDROOM - NIGHT

Hunter tosses and turns in his bed,
the images of the things these men
have told him dancing in front of his
eyes.

He can still hear the screams. Sleep
won't come.

Hunter gets out of bed and sits down
at his desk. He picks up a picture of
Captain McVay after his rescue. In the
old black and white picture, Captain
McVay looks haggard and haunted.

> HUNTER
> (VO)
> And they blamed captain
> McVay for it. They court
> martialed him.

INT - CAPTAIN MCVAY'S COURT MARTIAL

TITLE OVER:

December 4th, 1945
Building 57,
Washington naval yard

Captain McVay sits at the defense
table in a courtroom setting. A seven
man panel comprised of officers of
different ranks sits in judgment of
him.

The prosecuting Judge Advocate is
CAPTAIN THOMAS RYAN. He presents the
charges.

      RYAN
That you, by failing to
cause a zigzag course to be
steered in good visibility,
were negligent, and that you
were inefficient in the
performance of your duty.
That you failed to issue
timely orders to abandon
ship.

      HUNTER
   (VO)
They said it was his fault.

ON THE WITNESS STAND

Captain McVay answers the questions
put to him, maintaining his dignified
composure the whole time.

                 HUNTER
    The Captain told them what
    happened.

ON THE WITNESS STAND AGAIN

Bell takes the stand as does Twible,
McCoy, and other survivors, one after
the other.

                 HUNTER
                 (VO)
    So did the men who served
    under him. They all said
    what really happened.

ON THE WITNESS STAND

Mochitsura Hashimoto, commander of
the Japanese submarine, testifies.

                 HASHIMOTO
    We would have sunk that ship
    regardless of its course.

                    HUNTER
                (VO)
        Even the captain of the
        Japanese sub came forward
        and said that he would have
        sunk the Indianapolis
        anyway, but it didn't
        matter. Nothing anybody
        said was going to make any
        difference anyway.

A WIDER SHOT - THE COURT MARTIAL

Ryan stands before the panel,
speaking as the mouthpiece for them,
and for the whole of the Navy, as he
pronounces Captain McVay to be
guilty.

                    RYAN
        Guilty of negligence by
        failing to zigzag.

Standing in the face of his judgment,
Captain McVay falters only slightly.

                    RYAN (CONT'D)
        Guilty of failing to carry
        out your duty by failing to
        give the order to abandon
        ship in a timely manner, and
        by failing to ensure that a
        distress signal was sent.

Captain McVay is crushed, but maintains his composure. This is the judgment of his superiors, and he will have to accept that.

The spectators and participants file out of the court martial room. Captain McVay still sits at the defendants table.

Captain Ryan goes over to him.

                    RYAN (CONT'D)
          Charlie, you and I were
          classmates together. You
          know this is nothing
          personal, my friend.
          There's more to it then you
          and me. You have to know
          that.

                    MCVAY
          I know it, Tom. It's for the
          good of the Navy.

Captain McVay's voice breaks a little while he says it. He means the words, but it still hurts to say them.

Ryan claps McVay on the shoulder in a gesture of small comfort, then leaves captain McVay sitting alone in the drawing shadows of the empty courtroom.

                    HUNTER (VO)
          In the questionnaires I sent
          to the survivors, there was
          one question I asked them
          all. I asked if they thought
          Captain McVay was to blame
          for the sinking of the
          Indianapolis. Every one of
          them said he wasn't. Every
          single one.

                              TITLE OVER:

                    SPRING 1997

INT - THE HISTORY FAIR - DAY

Hunter stands in front of his history
project at the county history fair.
His project is a display of pictures.
There are some pictures of the men
before and after the sinking, some of
the ship, and some taken at captain
McVay's court martial. There are
letters from the survivors, framed
and hung up, and notebooks full of
their answers to his questionnaires.
There are flow charts and maps and a
pair of shark's jaws - a stark
reminder of what happened to so many
of the men in the pictures.

                    HUNTER (VO)
          I became the first 6th
          grader to ever win both the
          school and county divisions
          of the history fairs with my
          project about the Indy and
          Captain McVay.

The press is heavily photographing
this staggering wealth of information
about the Indianapolis and her crew.
Hunter is photographed a lot, too.

                    HUNTER (VO) (CONT'D)
          I was so happy! I thought
          that with so many people
          seeing the project, it might
          really help bring attention
          to the fight of the
          survivors of the
          Indianapolis to clear their
          captain of the court martial
          that he didn't deserve. I
          really felt like it could
          have made a difference.
          Until…

                              TITLE OVER

MAY 1977

INT. THE STATE HISTORY FAIR - DAY

The auditorium where the state
history fair finale is being held
bustles with activity. Rows and rows

of history projects are being looked
over by hundreds, maybe thousands of
people. The lights overhead are
bright, and the bustle of
conversation is lively. There are
press taking pictures of all of the
projects and talking to participants.

Hunter is standing in front of his
project when a woman approaches him
and bends to speak into his ear.
Hunter looks a little confused. The
woman points off to the side and he
looks in that direction.

He leaves the large, open auditorium
and goes down a hall full of people
toward where a sign by the door says
the interview part of the judging
process is being held.

INT - INTERVIEW ROOM

Hunter enters and is faced by three
judges.

                    JUDGE 1
          Name and project?

                    HUNTER
          Hunter Scott, Sir. My
          project is the triumph over
          tragedy of the survivors of
          the USS Indianapolis, which
          was sunk at the end of World
          War Two.

                    JUDGE 2
        Scott? I'm sorry son. We
        can't interview you.

                    HUNTER
        Sir?

                    JUDGE 1
        I'm sorry, Mr. Scott. You
        have to go.

Without any further discussion,
Hunter is ushered out of the room and
back to the auditorium.

Visibly shaken and confused, Hunter
begins to cry.

                    HUNTER
                 (VO)
        I didn't know what was going
        on. Why wouldn't they talk
        to me? What did I do wrong?

INT - THE STANDS

Alan Scott sees that something is
wrong with Hunter. He leaves the
stands and goes to where his son is.

INT - THE AUDITORIUM

Hunter and Alan find an easel standing
in front of his project display. On it
is a blown up page of the rules of

history fair competition. Parts of it
are highlighted.

It reads:

"Notebooks are not to be displayed
with the project."

                    HUNTER
        I'm disqualified? For
        having notebooks? But the
        men who were ON that ship
        wrote these notes! I was
        told to include them because
        of the historical
        significance of that! How
        can they disqualify me for
        that?

                    ALAN
        Hunter, that was at the
        school and county level.
        Apparently they have
        different rules here.

                    HUNTER
        But that girl's display is
        nothing but ROCKS. What do
        rocks have to do with
        triumph over tragedy?

                    ALAN
        I'm sorry, son. We might not
        like it, and I know it hurts,
        but those are the rules.

Hunter looks at his father with his last few tears still wet on his cheeks.

Alan wipes the tears off his son's cheek.

INT - THE SCOTT HOUSE - DAY

Hunter puts down the phone. He looks very sad. He lingers for a moment with his fingertips touching the phone before he leaves the room.

EXT - THE SCOTT'S BACK PORCH - - DAY

Hunter comes out the back door and sits beside his father on the back porch steps.

                    ALAN
          Did you tell them?

Hunter nods his head dejectedly.

                    HUNTER
          Yes Sir. I called all of the
          survivors. It was hard but I
          told them all that I failed
          them.

Alan is touched by his son's self-deprecation.

                    ALAN
          Do you really believe that?

                    HUNTER
Yes Sir. I do. I let them all
down. They had so much faith
in me and I let them all
down.

                    ALAN
You know, son. The truest
test of a man's character is
what it takes to make him
quit.

Alan let his words settle in.

                    ALAN (CONT'D)
So what are you going to do
about it?

                    HUNTER
              (VO)
My dad was a dream maker for
me when I needed it the most.

Alan gets up, leaving it at that.
Hunter has to decide for himself how
best to apply it.

                    HUNTER (CONT'D)
              (VO)
That's what the survivors
told me, too. Not to quit. I
guess if anybody knows about
not giving up, it's them.

EXT - CONGRESSMAN SCARBOROUGH'S OFFICE
BUILDING - DAY

Hunter and his father carry boxes from
the car into the large building.

                              TITLE OVER:

               A week later

               HUNTER
          (VO)
     A week later, I got a call
     from a member of our church.
     He said he had an office
     where a lot of people came
     and went, and he asked if we
     wanted to display my history
     project there.

INT CONGRESSMAN SCARBOROUGH'S OFFICE

Congressman Scarborough meets Hunter
and Alan. He shakes Alan's hand, then
Hunters, and ushers them to the area
where Hunter would be welcome to set
up his display.

               HUNTER
     His name was Joe
     Scarborough. Florida's
     republican congressman from
     the first district. When he
     said a lot of people would
     see my project, he meant it.

Ext. ON THE NEWSSTANDS - DAY

Pensacola News Journal papers get
stacked onto newsstands in grocery
stores, corner mailboxes, and gas
stations. Papers fall onto people's
front yards.

On the cover, the headline reads:

SHIP BECOMES STUDENT'S MISSION
A middle school history fair project
that seeks to correct history.

            HUNTER
      (VO)
  One of the people who heard
  about it was Steve Mraz. He
  was a reporter for the
  Pensacola News Journal.

INT - SCHOOL - DAY

Hunter is walking down the hall at
school between classes with his
backpack over one shoulder and some
books propped in one arm. He's the
picture of casual academics.

Students rush Hither and yon to get to
their next class.

A pretty girl waves at Hunter with a
smile.

                    PRETTY GIRL
          Hi, Hunter.

Hunter smiles easily and says hi back.

A boy, presumably a friend of Hunters,
catches up with him in the hallway.

                    BOY
          Hey, boat-boy. I saw your
          story in the paper. That's
          pretty cool.

Hunter notices that a good many people
are shooting him smiles and waves.
Apparently they think it's cool too.

                    HUNTER
          The next day, the story went
          out over the Associated
          Press. Papers picked it up
          across the country. Even
          Hawaii.

INT - BELL'S HOUSE

Mr. Bell comes in his door with his
mail in one hand and a newspaper under
his arm. He puts the mail on the table
beside his favorite recliner, sits
down, and shakes the paper open. On
the cover of the newspaper is the
story about Hunter and the
Indianapolis.

Mr. Bell smiles his approval and looks at the article for a moment before he picks up the phone.

EXT - HAWAII - A STREET CORNER NEWSSTAND - DAY

A man in a bright Hawaiian shirt picks up a copy of the paper. He looks at it with shocked disbelief. He doesn't even take his eyes off it to fish some money out of his pocket to pay for it.

                    HUNTER
          One of the newspapers that
          carried the article was the
          Litchfield times, in
          Connecticut. Captain McVay
          lived there before he died.
          Tom Brokaw lived there too.

INT - TOM BROKAW'S HOUSE

Tom Brokaw is reading the morning paper. He puts down his coffee, picks up the phone and dials. He keeps the paper in the other hand so he can keep reading it while he talks.

                    TOM BROKAW
          Hi. It's Tom. Listen, have
          you read the article in this
          morning's paper? No. The one
          about the boy and the
          battleship. No?
                    (MORE)

Well read it. I think this
kid is perfect for the piece
I'm doing on "The American
spirit." Yeah. This little
kid from nowhere is trying
to overturn a fifty year-old
court martial. Okay, let's
get on it.

                    TITLE OVER:

           July 30, 1997
        Indianapolis, Illinois

EXT - DOWNTOWN INDIANAPOLIS - DAY

There's a parade for the survivors of
the USS Indianapolis. There are
police cars, high school marching
bands, and some fire trucks. Hunter is
riding on the first fire truck,
smiling and waving to people along the
route along with several of the more
ambulatory survivors.

A cart with a camera crew follows
Hunter's progress.

EXT - THE SURVIVOR'S MONUMENT

Proudly, the men of the Indianapolis
march in procession toward the
memorial. In the middle of them,
Hunter walks proudly. He is the only
non-survivor allowed to walk with the
survivors at the memorial service.

NEARBY

The camera crew advances as far as
they are allowed. They film what they
are able from this respectable
distance.

AT THE MEMORIAL

Hunter steps forward alone and gently
places a flower at the base of the
memorial.

He reaches out his hand and traces his
fingers along the names etched there.
It is a little hand touching a big
piece of history.

The survivors watch him, humble not
only in the face of the memorial,
which they honor, but also in light of
Hunter's presence in front of it.
There are tears in the eyes of many of
them.

Hunter turns to them, and there are
tears in his eyes, too.

INT - THE SURVIVORS REUNION

Inside, the room is full of men
ranging in age from their sixties to
their eighties, their wives, and
other family and friends. Some of the
men have walkers, and some are in
wheelchairs.

Many of the older men are wearing
jackets, shirts, or caps that show
them to be survivors of the
Indianapolis.

Hunter mingles among the men easily,
wearing a tee shirt made for him,
which identifies him as a supporter of
the Indy and her crew's efforts to
clear Captain McVay.

WOODY JAMES notices the cameras that
are recording them, and pats Hunter
approvingly on the arm.

                    WOODY JAMES
          e don't pretend to try to
          look like heroes, but this
          kind of publicity just might
          shed enough light on the
          shadows of the injustice the
          Navy did to captain McVay.
          Shine enough light, you know
          there's nowhere for the
          shadows to hide.

                    COX
          You might just get this
          thing done, son.

                    HUNTER
          I hope so, Sir.

A man steps forward, extends his hand
to Hunter, and introduces himself.

                    QUATRO
          Hello, Hunter my name is
          Charles Butler McVay the
          fourth. You can call me
          Quatro. Everybody does.

Hunter and Quatro shake hands.

The camera crew makes sure to capture
these moments.

                    HUNTER
          Why do they call you that?

                    QUATRO
          Because I'm the 4th man in
          line and our family with
          that name. Quatro means four
          in Spanish.

Hunter nods. Oh, Of course.

                    HUNTER
          Yes Sir

                    QUATRO
          I admit I'm still angry at
          the way the Navy treated my
          father. Like any son should
          be, I'm proud of my father.
          Like the men here, I have
          tried for years to vindicate
          him. We never had any luck.
          I'm proud of you for what
          you're doing. Thank you.

                    HUNTER
        I'm happy to help, sir.

Eventually it comes time to leave.
Hunter looks admiringly after them.

                    HUNTER (CONT'D)
        I was met and welcomed by men
        I had only written letters
        with. It was like being in a
        room full of grandfathers.
        They became my heroes. Each
        and every one of them.

INT - THE SCOTT HOME

Hunter and his family are seated in
the living room in front of the
television, waiting for a show to
start.

                        TITLE OVER:

        August 1st, 1997

On the television screen, the nightly
news begins with Tom Brokaw
introducing the topic of the show.

                    TOM BROKAW
        Tonight we will look into
        stories that demonstrate
        "The American spirit.
                    (MORE)

Starting off, here is the incredible
story of a young man's crusade to
correct an injustice that began over
five decades ago. Hunter Scott…

The Scotts watch the segment, which
features the survivor's reunion and
Hunters crusade to clear Captain
McVay's name.

INT - KIMO MCVAY'S HOUSE - - DAY

A man in a bright Hawaiian shirt tunes
in his television set. This is the
same man who read the newspaper when
Hunter was the headline.

On the television screen is the same
broadcast of the NBC nightly news with
Tom Brokaw.

Kimo sits forward and pays close
attention.

                    TOM BROKAW
          …Is trying to clear the name
          of Captain Charles Butler
          McVay, who was court
          martialed after his ship,
          the USS Indianapolis, was
          sunk by a Japanese
          submarine…

The man in the bright shirt makes an
approving sound in his throat.

INT - THE SCOTT HOUSE - MORNING

The Scott family goes about the
business of getting started with the
day. Hunter and his sister eat
breakfast and stuff books into
backpacks, getting ready for school.
Alan gathers papers into his leather
bag and searches for his keys.
Hunter's mother, as all mothers do,
manages the rush.

Nearly constantly, the phone rings.

Once, Mrs. Scott will pick it up, give
a brief statement and hang up again.
Next, it might be Mr. Scott, or
Hunter.

Hunter's sister just looks confused
about why the phone's ringing so much.

The next time the phone rings, Hunter
picks it up, seemingly prepared to
hang up quickly. However, when he
hears what the person on the other end
has to say, he holds the phone closer
and listens.

Hunter listens for a second, then
calls for his father.

                HUNTER
     Dad? It's captain McVay's
     son.

                    ALAN
        Quatro?

                    HUNTER
        No Sir. He says his name is
        Kimo. He is inviting us to
        come visit him. In Hawaii.

Hunter's mother and sister look at
each other making impressed
"Oooooooh" faces.

Alan makes an approving face, too. One
that suggests that a trip to Hawaii
might not entirely be a hardship. He
takes the phone and talks to the man
on the other end.

HAWAII - DAYTIME

The sunshine is brilliant and the
foliage is bright and tropical, even
more so than Florida. Hunter and his
family climb out of a cab and approach
a wonderfully Hawaiian looking home.

                    TITLE OVER:

              Spring, 1998
                Hawaii

EXT - KIMO'S LANAI

While Hunter's mother, father, and
sister frolic at the swimming pool,

Captain McVay's son Kimo takes Hunter
inside his den.

Alan watches his son go inside the
house.

INT - KIMO'S DEN

There are bundles of letters held
together with string or rubber bands.
Kimo points them out to Hunter.

          KIMO
My father got those until he
died. They're from the
families of the men who
died. They blamed my father
for it and made sure he never
forgot it. Most of those
came during the holidays,
when they missed their loved
ones the most. Just like I
do.

FLASHBACK

In a room decorated brightly for
Christmas, Captain McVay opens cards
that have come. He reads each of them.

We HEAR what he reads, the voices of
the families who blame Captain McVay
for the people they love who died. The
voices was overlap, some filled with
the emotion of heartbroken loss. Some
are filled with vindictive anger.

                    VOICES OF BLAME
          Christmas doesn't matter
          anymore. You ruined
          Christmas forever. You
          killed my son. It should
          have been you who died, not
          him. The CAPTAIN is supposed
          to go down with the ship, not
          my son. How can you live with
          yourself, knowing my son
          died because of you? How can
          you sleep? Why don't you
          just kill yourself?

                    HUNTER
          I don't understand how
          people could be so cruel. It
          must have been horrible.

The captain's wife comes into the
room, sees what Captain McVay is
doing, and becomes gently angered.
She takes the cards from him and tears
them in half before throwing them
down. She kneels beside him on the
sofa and holds him to her.

                    MRS. MCVAY
          Pay them no mind, my love.
          Pay them no mind.

INT - KIMO'S DEN

Kimo sees that Hunter is upset, and
draws the boy's attention away from
the letters.

                    KIMO
But my father never blamed
any of the families. He
understood what it was like
to lose those men. He lost
them, too.

On the coffee table is a little toy
soldier. Hunter notices it and asks
Kimo about it.

                    HUNTER
Oh, does that belong to your
children?

Kimo sits down and waves at the space
next to him in an invitation for
Hunter to do the same.

                    KIMO
That belonged to my father.
It was given to him when he
was a young boy.

FLASHBACK

In a hazy, faraway flashback, a large
man in a very impressive uniform with
a great many medals, braids and
ribbons on it, leans forward with the
toy in his white gloved hand.

                    THE UNIFORMED MAN'S VOICE
          This is for you, Charlie.
          You'll be a great captain
          one day, too. And you'll
          take good care of your
          soldiers, won't you, son?

     A young boy takes it and smiles
     brightly, thankfully.

                    CHARLIE
          Yes Sir! Thanks, dad!

     The gloved hand tussles little
     Charlie's hair.

     In the present, KIMO continues.

                    KIMO
          My father was holding that
          the day he died.

                              TITLE OVER:

               Litchfield CT
               November 6th, 1968

     EXT - MCVAY'S FARM - DAY

     Outside a lovely but modest house,
     behind which two sturdy barns stand
     sentry - a fading hex sign adorning
     one - Captain McVay, now in his
     sixties, and his gardener are

insulating bushes for the coming
winter.

INT - MCVAY KITCHEN - DAY

FLORENCE REGOSIA looks out the
kitchen window and sees Captain McVay
and his hired man headed toward one of
the barns.

She goes to the door and yells out.

                    FLORENCE
          Cap! Your lunch is in here
          waiting for you! Best come
          have it before it goes cold!

Captain McVay waves his pending
compliance, says a few words to the
gardener and turns in the direction of
the house. His hired man continues
into the barn.

Satisfied that she's being obeyed,
Florence goes about the rest of her
household duties.

EXT - THE MCVAY DRIVEWAY

Thunder rolls in the distance and
captain McVay pauses in the driveway
between the barns and the house.

A sharp Thunder clap causes captain
McVay to stop cold. He doesn't just
hear the Thunder clap. He also hears

the explosions from when the torpedoes hit and sank his ship.

With that sound comes a flood of other sounds and the memories that come with them.

             SOUNDS
    Men screaming, metal
    tearing away from metal,
    explosions, rushing water,
    and still more screams.

Captain McVay hitches a breath, overwhelmed.

INT - MCVAY KITCHEN - DAY

Florence returns to the kitchen to find the captain's lunch untouched. She mutters her displeasure.

             FLORENCE
    If I told that man once, I
    told him a hundred times…

Florence glances out the back door, prepared to chastise Captain McVay if she sees him loitering there. He is not. The driveway is empty.

INT - MCVAY STAIRCASE - DAY

Florence climbs the stairs, muttering all the way.

                    FLORENCE
         All right, so you're in your
         room, then. I told you your
         lunch would go cold and now
         it has. And what will I do
         about it?

Florence sighs heavily.

                    FLORENCE (CONT'D)
         I will warm it for you like
         I always do.

INT MCVAY'S BEDROOM - DAY

Florence finds Captain McVay's door
ajar and lets herself into his room.

On McVay's bed, some bundles of
letters lay open and undone. Some
letters lie loose, unfolded on the
bedspread.

                    FLORENCE
         What in the world…?

Florence's gaze falls on a holster on
the night table. There is no gun in it.

EXT - MCVAY BACK DOOR - DAY

Florence comes bounding out the back
door, calling for the captain.

Rain has begun to fall.

EXT - MCVAY FRONT YARD - DAY

Captain McVay stands on his front
lawn, and lets the rain fall on him.
Silhouetted against the Gray November
sky, he HEARS the roar of rushing
water and the horrible rending of
metal from metal. In his mind, scenes
play out from the night of the
sinking. Most of all, he HEARS the
agonized screams of his men as they
suffer and die around him.

EXT - THE DRIVEWAY AROUND BACK - DAY

The hired man hears Florence yelling
and comes out of the barn to see what
she's on about. They no sooner meet in
the middle of the driveway than we
HEAR a shot ring out.

Both Florence and the hired man look
toward the front of the house,
horrified.

EXT - MCVAY FRONT YARD - DAY

Florence and the hired man come
rushing from the back yard and find
Captain McVay laying in his front
yard. Florence shrieks and the hired
man turns her away by her shoulders so
she won't see any more.

                    HIRED MAN
          Florence, go call 911.
          Hurry!

Florence, shaken and sobbing, goes.

With Florence inside, the hired man
rushes to captain McVay.

In his hand, Captain McVay is holding
a toy soldier, the same one that was
given to him as a child.

INT - KIMO'S DEN - PRESENT DAY

Kimo is holding the toy soldier in his
own hand.

                    KIMO
          My father didn't really
          survive after all. The Indy
          sank in fourteen minutes. It
          took twenty-three years and
          three months for my father
          to follow her down.

Kimo puts the toy soldier on the table
and smiles at Hunter, then pats him on
the shoulder. Brought together by the
memory of Captain McVay, these two
understand each other.

INT - KIMO'S KITCHEN - DAY

The Scott family is scattered around
the kitchen, either having something
to drink or sitting at the table
munching on sandwiches or fruit.

Kimo comes into the room carrying a
few things. He sits down at the
kitchen table with Hunter and puts the
things down in front of them.

The items include a large packet of
papers, a flip-open lighter, a
plaque, and a set of dog tags.

                    KIMO
          These things are for you.

The Scott family gathers around to
look.

Kimo hands over the lighter. Hunter
takes it reverently.

                    KIMO (CONT'D)
          This lighter was given to my
          father at the first
          survivor's reunion in
          nineteen sixty.

Kimo gives Hunter the plaque.

                    KIMO (CONT'D)
          This plaque was given to me
          when the memorial was
          dedicated in 1990, since my
          father wasn't alive by then.

Kimo puts the dog tags into Hunter's
hand, then Kimo turns one dog tag
over. On the back of it is his father's
thumbprint. Hunter gapes at it.

                    KIMO (CONT'D)
          These were my father's dog
          tags at the Academy. There's
          his thumbprint on the back.

Hunter looks dumbfounded.

                    HUNTER
          I can't keep these. There
          are two important.

                    KIMO
          Yes you can. I think he would
          be very happy for you to have
          them. I know he's smiling
          down on you and saying "Well
          done, young man."

Hunter closes his hand around the dog
tags. He is obviously deeply moved.

Kimo slides the papers over to Hunter.

                    KIMO (CONT'D)
These are papers that you
will probably find useful.
I'm passing the torch to
you, Hunter. The survivors
have tried for fifty years
to clear my father, and so
have I. It's easy for the
Navy to ignore those men.
They're loyal and they're
biased. Of course they're
going to defend him. I'm
easy to dismiss, too. He was
my father. But you. You're
different. You're not so
easy to ignore. You've
gotten farther in a few
months than I have in half a
century. We're pinning our
hopes on you now.

                    HUNTER
                 (VO)
The things he gave me are the
most precious items in my
Indianapolis collection.
They make me feel closer to
captain McVay. It is a
strange feeling to feel so
close to someone you've
never met. But the men of the
Indianapolis are my heroes,
and the captain is probably
the most highly esteemed of
those.

Kimo grins at Hunter, and asks him:

                    KIMO
          Are you ready to take a ride?

                    HUNTER
          Sure!

EXT - AT THE SHORE - DAY

Hunter, his family, and Kimo are
standing on a dock beside a very large
submarine. They are met by commander
Toti.

                    TOTI
          Hello. I'm commander Toti,
          and this is the
          Indianapolis, named for
          your captain's ship. Would
          you like a ride?

                    HUNTER
          You bet!

INT - THE INDIANAPOLIS SUB

Hunter is escorted through the sub to
the command deck, where he looks
around with fascination. The crew is
sharp, and makes a pointed effort to
be courteous to Hunter and his family.

TOPSIDE

The sub cruises near the shore, giving
Hunter a ride standing with commander
Toti and Kimo.

Hunter can't contain his excitement.
Hunter grins wide.

                HUNTER
    I felt more resolved than
    ever that when I grow up, I
    want to join the Navy.

EXT - KIMO'S HOUSE

Kimo escorts the Scotts to a taxi.

While the cabbie helps put the bags in
the trunk, and Mrs. Scott bundles
Hunter's sister into the car, Kimo
takes Hunter and Alan aside. He gives
Alan a business card.

                KIMO
    This is the number of a man
    I've known a long time. His
    name is Mike Monroney, and
    he's listed in many
    publications as one of the
    hundred most influential
    people in Washington. I
    talked to him about you and
    he wants to meet you and
    Hunter.

Alan takes the card.

                    ALAN
          Thank you. We'll call him.

Hunter and Kimo begin to say goodbye
with a handshake but decide on a hug
instead.

Hunter and Alan get in the car. Kimo
waves at it as it pulls away from the
curb and leaves.

                    TITLE OVER:

     Third week of April 1988

INT - MIKE MONRONEY'S OFFICE

Hunter and Alan enter the office and
shake hands with Mr. Monroney. He is
an older man, his age comparable to
the ages of the survivors with whom
Hunter's met.

They all sit

                    MONRONEY
          I hear impressive things
          about you, young man.

                    HUNTER
          I hear good things about
          you, Mr. Monroney.

MONRONEY

What a dear boy. Hunter, do
you know why I was willing to
come out of retirement and
help you with this bill? Did
Kimo McVay tell you that?

HUNTER

No Sir. He didn't.

Mr. Monroney takes a picture out of
his wallet and hands it across to
Hunter. It's a wallet-size picture of
a young sailor in his Navy whites,
like the pictures of sailors that
Hunter has as part of his history fair
display.

MONRONEY

In July, nineteen
forty-five, I was stricken
with a horrible flu. It kept
me from sailing out with my
ship. If I hadn't been sick,
I would have been aboard the
Indianapolis when she sank.
So, you see, this is a
subject I take very
personally.

Hunter examines the picture, and
looks at Mr. Monroney with a new
measure of respect.

Monroney can't help but notice
Hunters frank admiration. He smiles
warmly in the face of it, and
continues.

                MONRONEY (CONT'D)
     Let me tell you what amazes
     me about you. Usually people
     have to go in search of the
     press to get their
     attention, but in your case,
     the media come looking for
     you. I've never seen
     anything like it.

Mr. Monroney draws a breath,
considering his words before he
proceeds.

                MONRONEY (CONT'D)
     I cannot stress to you
     enough the importance and
     effective use that the media
     can play. It's easy to say no
     to somebody over the phone,
     or by letter. But, with a boy
     as well informed,
     charismatic, appealing and
     frankly as young as Hunter
     is, it's much harder to say
     no. Especially when there's
     a camera making sure
     everybody in America could
     be watching.

Hunter nods. that makes perfect
sense.

                HUNTER
     They can be sneaky, they
     just don't want anybody to
     see them doing it.

                MONRONEY
     I think you have a very good
     understanding of politics,
     my young friend.

Hunter and Alan laugh.

                MONRONEY (CONT'D)
     I've made some appointments
     for you to meet with a lot of
     people who can help. The
     more we can get on our side,
     the better.

                HUNTER
     I understand, Sir. I'm
     ready.

INT - THE HALLWAY SOMEWHERE ON CAPITAL HILL

Speaker of the house, Newt Gingrich,
shakes hands with Hunter, smiling for
the camera.

With the camera rolling Hunter boldly
asks:

                    HUNTER
        Mr. Gingrich, can we count
        on your support for joint
        resolution, twenty-six?

Mr. Gingrich smiles, and it appears to
be a genuine one.

                    GINGRICH
        Not only that, young man.
        I'm very impressed with you.
        You've got a summer job if
        you want it.

                    HUNTER
        I'm sure my father will say
        I'm too young for that right
        now, but thank you for
        letting me talk with you.

In other hallways, with other cameras
watching, different politicians
shake hands with Hunter. All of them
are smiling, except one who frowns in
the face of the camera and closes the
door in Hunter's face.

INT - ROBERT SMITH'S OFFICE

ROBERT SMITH shake Hunter's hand,
then watches Hunter leave, taking the
cameras with him.

Smith's secretary comes in with the
mail.

                    SECRETARY
          What was that all about?

                    SMITH
          That was a very impressive
          young man. I just told him I
          was going to support his
          crusade. But I think I can do
          better than that. He said he
          was working with Mike
          Monroney. Get his number for
          me.

Smith sits down at his desk, rubs his
chin a few times, thinking, then picks
up a pen. He begins to quickly scratch
out some notes on a pad.

When the phone rings, Smith picks it
up.

                    SMITH (CONT'D)
          Thanks, Helen. Yeah, put me
          through.

There is a pause.

                    SMITH (CONT'D)
          Mr. Monroney? Hi. This is
          senator Bob Smith. If you
          have the time, I'd like to
          talk to you.

                              TITLE OVER:

          January 1998

INT - SCARBOROUGH'S OFFICE - NIGHT

Congressman Scarborough, Mike
Monroney, and senator Smith are in
Scarborough's office. With coffee
cups strewn about and fast food
containers abandoned on the table, it
looks like they've been there for a
while.

                SCARBOROUGH
        What's wrong with it now?

                SMITH
        As far as I'm concerned,
        nothing. But this is a bill
        that we're going to push in
        front of the Senate Arms
        Committee, if we can get one
        convened. And you know how
        damned picky they're going
        to be about the wording.

                MONRONEY
        Right. We are going to have
        to concede that,
        technically, the court
        martial wasn't about the
        ship sinking.

                SMITH
        We all know that's bull. It
        wasn't about anything else.

                    MONRONEY
         But not on paper. On PAPER,
         it's about technical
         details nobody understands.
         They're only going to try to
         confuse the issue with a lot
         of double-talk about
         visibility and weather and
         crap like that.

                    SCARBOROUGH
         All right, if we can't say
         it's about the sinking, how
         can we word it?

The men settle into more debate.

EXT - PENSACOLA HIGH FOOTBALL FIELD - NIGHT

There is a high school football game
going on. People in the stands throw
popcorn, clap with the cheerleaders,
and munch on hot dogs.

Hunter plays center forward on his
football team. On a particularly
successful drive, Hunter's team
advances the ball. People in the
stands cheer their approval.

                         TITLE OVER:

April 1998

EXT. THE CAPITAL BUILDING - DAY

Hunter, Mike Monroney, congresswoman
Julia Carson, Kimo, congressman
Scarborough, Mike Monroney, several
other people in suits, and the
survivors stand in a group, getting
ready to face a horde of television
cameras and crews.

Behind them is a sharp and impressive
view of the capitol building, in front
of which they're standing.

With everything settled, on cue, the
group put on their game faces and
advances toward the stand of
microphones.

                    HUNTER
          I had never seen so many
          television cameras in my
          life.

Congresswoman Julia Carson steps
forward and speaks with a frank,
authoritative tone.

                    CARSON
          It is my privilege to, along
          with my distinguished
          colleagues, introduce Joint
          House resolution 26.
                    (MORE)

It is the intention of this legislature, if it is passed, to exonerate Captain Charles Butler McVay the third of charges brought against him in court martial following the sinking of his ship, the USS Indianapolis. That court martial constitutes an injustice of enormous magnitude, and the time for it to be rectified is long overdue. This resolution was brought about due to the efforts of Hunter Scott, a fine young man whose search for justice has brought all of us together. Mr. Scott himself will drop the resolution into the hopper.

Applause shows that a few people actually have been listening.

While congresswoman Carson and the other grown politicians are all well versed, being the people who drafted the bill, the attention of the reporters focuses on Hunter. The press clamors for answers from him and jostle to get good pictures of him.

REPORTER
Hunter! What do you want to be when you grow up?

                    HUNTER
          I want to go into the Naval
          Academy, and I want to be an
          officer.

Congresswoman Carson graciously
accepts the shunning of the press.
Likewise, the others, including the
survivors present, all simply smile
in the background. They knew the focus
would be on Hunter, and are fine with
it.

Whatever it takes to get attention for
the bill.

                    ANOTHER REPORTER
          Hunter! Why is this so
          important to you?

                    HUNTER
          I just want to give honor
          back to these men, to whom
          honor means so much.

With that, congresswoman Carson, Mike
Monroney, and the others close ranks
around Hunter and usher him off in the
direction of the building.

EXT - AT THE DOOR

As they try to enter the building, a
guard stops them.

                    GUARD
     I'm sorry. There are no
     children allowed past this
     point.

Congresswoman Carson doesn't skip a
beat. Even though she is an African
American, and Hunter is Caucasian,
she puts her hand protectively on
Hunter's shoulder.

                    CARSON
     It's all right. He's my son.

She ushers Hunter inside quickly,
leaving the guard flabbergasted.

The guard briefly considers saying
something else, and then quickly
thinks better of it. He recovers his
position and lets them pass.

                         TITLE OVER:

September 13th, 1999

INT - PENSACOLA HIGH - MUD ROOM

The Pensacola high football team is
coming off the field from practice.

His coach stop Hunter, who is still
dressed in his football uniform as he
enters the mud room.

                    COACH
Hunter, congratulations on
being elected class
president today. This is
your third year in a row,
isn't it?

                    HUNTER
Thank you, Sir. Yes it is.

                    COACH
Is it true that you're going
out of town again?

                    HUNTER
Yes, Sir. I'm going to speak
at the Senate arms committee
tomorrow.

                    COACH
Hunter, I don't like having
to do this, but if you miss
two more practices, I have
to keep you out of the game
on Friday.

Hunter looks disappointed, but he
doesn't hesitate.

                    HUNTER
I understand, Sir. But I
have to do this. It's
important.

                    COACH
     I know that what you're
     doing is really important,
     but these are the rules, and
     they have to apply to
     everyone equally.

Hunter nods. He does understand the
concept very well.

                    HUNTER
     Yes, Sir.

His coach claps him on the shoulder
pad.

                    COACH
     Good man.

                         TITLE OVER:

Tuesday, September 14TH 1999 9:30 AM
Room SH-216, Hart Senate Office
Building

INT - INSIDE THE COMMITTEE HEARING

The room is largely full, with a lot
of Navy officers and press and
attendance. Prominent in the front
are the survivors of the USS
Indianapolis. They are each wearing a
blue satin jacket with a picture of
the Indianapolis on the back, with ten
stars above that.

Beneath the hull number, CA- 35. There
is the inscription "Still at sea"
embroidered in gold. The survivors
are also wearing baseball caps with
gold trim. Each man's cap is adorned
with his own medals pinned to it, and
a picture of the Indy on the front. On
the back, embroidered in gold
lettering is the word survivor.

The survivors still have their caps
on. Ordinarily, military men remove
their head coverings when indoors.
But, if anybody has earned the right
to wear their badges of courage
inside, they have.

Senator JOHN WARNER, chairman of the
Senate Armed Services Committee and
former secretary of the Navy, is the
last one to arrive.

Senator Warner settles into his
position in the center of the panel,
and begins to speak.

                    WARNER
          We are here to remember the
          sinking of the USS
          Indianapolis, but more
          significantly to remember
          the courage of those who were
          aboard the ship that fateful
          night, and particularly
          those who are here with us
          today.

Every head in the room turns to look
at the survivors in the room. They
bear the scrutiny well, with dignity,
their heads held high. This moment in
court, with the hopes of finally
clearing their captain, is what
they've waited a long time for. If
people wanted to look, let them.

                WARNER (CONT'D)
    I now introduce senator Bob
    Smith.

Alert and ready, senator Smith
begins.

                SMITH
    The sinking of the USS
    Indianapolis was one of the
    greatest tragedies in U.S.
    Naval history. You're
    probably familiar with the
    story. The Indianapolis
    delivered the bomb that got
    dropped on Hiroshima. The
    Indianapolis was sunk, and
    the brave survivors endured
    an ordeal at sea that the
    rest of us cannot begin to
    imagine. And then there was
    a court martial.
                (MORE)

Two Admirals, Nimitz and
Spruance, said it shouldn't
happen, and afterwards,
secretary of the Navy
Forrestal remitted the
sentence. That can easily be
interpreted as an admission
that the trial was unjust. I
am not an historical
revisionist. Neither are
the survivors, and neither
is Hunter Scott. We don't
want to rewrite history. We
just want to set the record
straight. Today, thanks
largely to the efforts of
Hunter Scott, there is new
information that wasn't
available at the court
martial or any of the
subsequent investigations.
There is NEW evidence that I
would ask this committee and
the senate to listen very
carefully to.

He pauses for a moment, for effect.

                    SMITH (CONT'D)
          Let's meet the men we're
          talking about. Gentlemen,
          would you introduce
          yourselves?

One by one, the survivors stand, the
ones who can, and introduce
themselves. Every person in

attendance regards them with no small
measure of awe.

                    MURPHY
          My name is Paul J. Murphy of
          Broomfield, Co. I am a
          survivor of the USS
          Indianapolis. With your
          permission I would like to
          submit a lengthy and
          definitive statement for
          the record, as well as
          statements from other
          survivors who could not be
          here.

                    WARNER
          You may do so without
          objection.

                    TWIBBLE
          My name is Harlan Twibble,
          and I served as an Ensign
          aboard the USS
          Indianapolis. I testified
          at captain McVay's court
          martial just as I'm
          testifying here. We, all of
          us, would like to ask this
          Congress to right the wrong
          to one of its nation's
          valiant warriors, captain
          Charles B. McVay.
                    (MORE)

We would ask the Congress to
remember that we were the
ship chosen to deliver the
vital component of the bomb
that helped end a horrible
war.

Mr. Twibble's voice floods with
emotion and falters just a little as
he continues.

                    TWIBBLE (CONT'D)
          We were a good ship, and we
          had a good captain. Thank
          you.

                    WARNER
          Ensign Twibble, in all my
          years here in the Senate, I
          cannot recall a more moving
          statement than you have just
          delivered. Thank you.

                    MCCOY
          I'm Giles McCoy, from
          Florida, and I was a PGC from
          the Marine Corps aboard the
          Indianapolis. We had
          thirty-nine marines aboard,
          and we did the security
          aboard ship. I want to
          explain what a combat
          veteran is.
                        (MORE)

A combat veteran is a person
that puts his life on the
line for his country. He
does this for the freedom of
his country, he does it for
the justice and honor of
serving his country. Even
though captain McVay died in
nineteen sixty-eight, HIS
honor is at stake. That's
why I'm here. That's why
we're all here.

                    WARNER
Sir, what are the ten stars
for on the back of your
jacket?

                    MCCOY
That one star for each
battle the Indianapolis
fought in.

                    WARNER
Thank you, Sir.

The survivors continue to introduce
themselves to a room that is absorbed
in hearing them.

                    MCGUIGGAN
I'm Bob McGuiggan. I was a
Gunners mate striker,
Fourth Division, on the
five-inch.
(MORE)

And a catapult Gunner's
mate. I came aboard the
Indianapolis in forty-two,
and spent nine invasion
operations with the
Indianapolis.

                KURYLA
Mike Kuryla, junior. I was a
coxswain aboard the ship,
Fourth Division, fourth
section, the five-inch
twenty-fives. I was
director of fire control.

                MINER
My name is Jack Miner, from
Northbrook, Illinois. I was
a radio technician, second-
class. My time aboard ship
was two weeks. That's all of
it.

Senator Smith allows a moment for both
the audience and the panel to fully
appreciate the moment. When he
speaks, he addresses the panel, the
audience, and the television cameras,
which are carefully recording this.

                SMITH
gentlemen, there is great
history here.

                    WARNER
          We would like to invite
          these survivors to come down
          here and take a seat right in
          the front row. They are at
          least as important as any
          other witness. I see that
          the sons of captain McVay,
          Charles B. McVay the fourth
          and Kimo McVay are also
          here. Would you also like to
          come forward? Thank you very
          much.

The survivors of the Indy come forward
and take seats in the front. So do the
sons of Captain McVay.

It takes a moment for the older men to
travel the distance to the front of
the room, but not one person present
tries to rush them. These men can take
as long as they need.

                 WARNER (CONT'D)
          Thank you very much. Now we
          will proceed. We have looked
          forward to this testimony
          for a long time. Mr. Scott.

Hunter is willing and quite able to
proceed. He delivers his statement
concisely.

                    HUNTER
Thank you, Mr. Chairman and
distinguished guests and
members of the Armed
Services Committee. Thank
you for allowing me the
opportunity to testify here
today in support of Senate
Joint Resolution
twenty-six. When their
captain was court
martialed, these men were
angered and outraged, and I
don't blame them. Captain
McVay survived the
nightmare too, struggling
to survive on the open sea,
listening to his men
suffering and dying all
around him. To hold him
responsible for it was just
not right.

Hunter takes a breath.

                    HUNTER (CONT'D)
Abraham Lincoln once said,
"The probability that we may
fail in the struggle ought
not to deter us from a cause
we believe to be just." I
began this just cause to
exonerate captain McVay and
to gain a Presidential Unit
Citation for the
Indianapolis and her crew.
                    (MORE)

What started out as a school history project has turned into a mission, a mission to right a wrong inflicted fifty-four years ago. I know you are here today because you believe deeply in American democracy. I am no different than you in this belief, and that is why I have journeyed here, as a representative from my heroes, the men of the Indianapolis. I have learned that democracy is a treasure so valued, men and women are willing to give their lives in its pursuit. I know eight hundred and eighty men of the USS Indianapolis made the supreme sacrifice. I pray that some of those who gave their lives are looking down on what I'm doing at this moment with a smile, knowing their sacrifice was not in vain.

                CHAIRMAN WARNER
That was a well delivered statement, young man.

                SENATOR SMITH
If I may?

                    CHAIRMAN WARNER
          Go ahead.

                    SENATOR SMITH
          Hunter Scott is too modest
          to say this, but I think it
          is important to point out
          that because he is missing
          practice to appear here
          today, Hunter won't be
          allowed to play in his next
          football game. This sends a
          message that Hunter Scott
          understands what is
          important in America. Too
          bad the coach doesn't.

Senator Smith turns slightly and
addresses Hunter.

                    SMITH
          Hunter, if you would like, I
          will write you a note.

Survivor Mr. Murphy is quick to raise
his hand.

                    MURPHY
          I'll write a Note too.

The room fills with appreciative
laughter.

Hunter smiles at both men.

                    HUNTER
          Thank you. I appreciate
          that.

Senator Smith begins to direct his
statements to Hunter.

                    SMITH
          Now, Mr. Scott. As a former
          teacher, let me say how much
          I admire and respect you for
          just getting your teeth into
          a project that you believe in.
          That is certainly admirable.
          You are certainly a source of
          inspiration to all of us, and
          certainly, hopefully, to the
          young people of America who
          may be watching, as well as a
          few of us older folks.

                    HUNTER
          Thank you.

                    SMITH
          I know that in your
          research, you found some
          documents that had not been
          discovered before. I want to
          ask you about one of them,
          the so called ULTRA
          document. Can you elaborate
          just briefly on what that
          was, and also indicate to
          this committee why that's
          significant?

                    HUNTER
Yes Sir. The Ultra -

                    SMITH
Speak into that microphone,
please. Pull it up closer.

                    HUNTER
The ULTRA document was top
secret during World War Two
period it wasn't brought in
captain McVay's trial. What
the ULTRA document is, it
was classified information
at the time, saying that the
United states Navy broke the
Japanese code and that they
knew that there were
submarines in the area. The
Navy new, by name, that the
I-58 and the K-367 were the
two closest submarines in
Captain McVay's path, but
they denied him his request
for an escort.

                    SMITH
So we have it on record that
Captain McVay specifically
asked for an escort ship?

                    HUNTER
Yes Sir, he did.
                    (MORE)

But the person in charge of
escorts was given
information that there were
no enemy Subs in the area. So
the Indianapolis became the
FIRST ship to sail that
route without an escort ship
even though she had no
submarine equipment. No
sonar, no nothing.

Hunter takes the chance to add another
bit of information before the subject
gets changed.

       HUNTER (CONT'D)
Reports also said that there
was no distress signal sent,
and that's not true.

Hunter turns to tell the next part to
chairman Warner.

       HUNTER (CONT'D)
"Jaws" was wrong about that
part, too.

The room fills with appreciative
chuckles. As solidly as Hunter is able
to deliver the facts, he is still a
young man with many of the endearing
qualities of a child.

Smith tactfully allows a moment for
Hunter's charm to soak into the room
before he continues.

                    SMITH
          This was also not introduced
          at the court martial, is
          that correct?

                    HUNTER
          Yes Sir. The official Navy
          version states that no SOS
          messages from the
          Indianapolis were received,
          but through my research I
          found that to be false. They
          were received in three
          different places.

                              TITLE OVER:

          July 29, 1945

INT - THE RADIO ROOM OF THE INDY

Miner is thrown from his chair in the
initial blast. He looked nervously
from the door to his radio panel.
Woods, still seated, orders him out.

                    WOODS
          You need to get out of here.
          Go get a life jacket on! Go!

Minor goes.

Despite having been burned, Woods
begins to send the distress signal.

A moment later, Orr rushes in.

                    ORR
We have to get a distress
message out right by God
now!

                    WOODS
I'm way ahead of you, Sir.

                    ORR
Out, now! We're abandoning
ship! Get out!

                         TITLE OVER:

LDI-1004 Harbor examination vessel
Leyte Gulf.

INT - VESSEL CABIN - NIGHT

Russell Hetz turns his attention to
the radio assembly when a distress
signal comes in saying that the
Indianapolis is going down after
being struck eight minutes earlier.

                    HETZ
They've been getting prank
reports from Japanese boats
like this. There's no way a
ship the size of the Indy can
go down that fast. Make a
note in the log.

```
                    TITLE OVER:


 Claire B. Young's post

 INT - POST - NIGHT

 Mr. Young is at his post when he
 receives a distress signal. He shucks
 off his headphones, rushes to the
 bathroom and knocks on the door.

                YOUNG'S BOSS
     Fuck off, Young. I'm still
     cropping out the tacos from
     Henry's Hacienda. Don't
     ever eat there, kid.

                YOUNG
     No Sir. I've got a distress
     call, here. It's…

                BOSS
     For fuck's sake, Young, my
     asshole is on fire in here.
     No reply at this time. If you
     get any further messages,
     come tell me.


                HUNTER
     Of course no further
     messages came. The ship was
     gone.
```

Don Alan's post

Don Alan is sitting at his post with
headphones on, when he receives the
distress signal.

> HUNTER (CONT'D)
> Seaman Don Alan heard the
> signal, too. His boss,
> Commodore Gillette, had
> given orders not to be
> disturbed because he was
> playing cards. So Mr. Alan
> took some initiative.

Seaman Alan rapidly flips through the
pages on a clipboard. He jabs his
finger on one page and keys his radio.

> HUNTER (CONT'D)
> He sent two seagoing tugs to
> go out and assist. Well,
> when Commodore Gillette got
> finished with his game and
> came back, he was angry that
> a junior officer gave an
> order like that. So he
> ordered the tugs to turn
> around and go back to port.

There is an audible gasp in the room.
This is the first public news that
there could have been a rescue the

first day, not the fifth. Nobody knew
that before.

Jack Miner gets tears in his eyes. He
whispers to himself.

                    MINER
          They did hear us.

Even the panelists look a bit agape.
Either they didn't know it or were
staggered that Hunter knew, and could
prove it.

                    SMITH
          Where did you get this
          research, Hunter?

                    HUNTER
          After I appeared on
          different TV shows, people
          would call me and tell me
          stuff. They sent me letters
          talking about it, and one of
          them sent me the ULTRA
          document.

                    SMITH
          So it is correct, then, that
          this information was not
          brought into the court
          martial. Is that correct?

                    HUNTER
        Yes Sir. It was classified
        top secret, so it was not
        used at the court martial of
        Captain McVay. It's been
        declassified since then.

                    SMITH
        That's pretty dramatic new
        information. Hunter is your
        evidence solid?

Hunter meets Senator Smith's eyes
evenly and doesn't waver in his
answer.

                    HUNTER
          As a rock, Sir.

Hunter pushes his research forward a
few inches, daring Smith or anybody
else to go through it if they want to.

The room fills with appreciative
laughter. Even the hardboiled panel
can appreciate this bold confidence,
and join the laughter.

Hunter, used to the attention, does
not falter. He's been ready for this
for a long time.

Chairman Warner smiles and invites
the proceedings to continue.

                    WARNER
We will hear from Rear
Admiral John Hutson, Judge
Advocate General Counsel of
the Navy.

                    HUTSON
Captain McVay's court
martial had nothing to do
with the sinking of his
ship, the USS Indianapolis.
Captain McVay was court
martialed for an error in
judgment, both that he
failed to zig zag, and that
he failed to send distress
message. Given the
information available at
the time, that the court
martial was fair.

                    WARNER
Thank you, Rear Admiral
Hutson. We will also hear
the statement of Admiral
Pilling, Vice Chief of Naval
operations, US Navy.

Pilling is bristled and confident.
He's been coached for this, and is
sure there's nothing they can throw at
him that he's not ready for.

PILLING
A commanding officer has
full accountability for his
ship and crew, and there is
no parallel for the
principle of accountability
in the command of a ship,
either in civilian life or
in other parts of the
military. Captain McVay had
absolute accountability for
his decisions and actions.
When those decisions were
examined by court martial of
experienced officers,
Captain McVay was found
guilty of an error in
professional judgment. I
firmly believe his trial was
fair. Captain McVay
understood these concepts
perfectly.

SMITH
Yes, he understood it, and
accepted it. He so loved the
Navy, and respected the
tradition, reputation, and
judgment of the Navy, that
he carried it with him to his
grave.

Senator Smith verbally confronts
Admiral Pilling that the court
martial was weak.

                    SMITH (CONT'D)
How many other captains of
any other vessel was ever
court martialed for the
sinking of his ship during
wartime?

                    PILLING
I wouldn't have that exact
number.

                    SMITH
Never mind an exact number.
Have ANY other captains ever
been court martialed
because their ship sank in
wartime?

Pilling pauses before he answers. He
knows what he's been coached to say,
but he also swore to tell the truth.

                    PILLING
No. None. But I repeat that
Captain McVay was not court
martialed for the sinking -

SENATOR SMITH CUTS HIM OFF

                    SMITH
    None.

A couple of men on the panel turn to
speak to each other in hushed tones
behind their hands. Likewise, people
in the gallery whisper to each other.

                    SMITH (CONT'D)
It is your position, and the
position of the Navy, that
captain McVay was court
martialed because of an
error in his judgment. For
decisions he made that
night. Is that right?

                    PILLING
That is correct.

                    SMITH
All right, let's look at
that, then. An error in his
judgment. Let me ask you
something. Was it an error
in judgment for captain
McVay not to have been
allowed an escort, when
there was intelligence of
enemy Subs in the area?

                    PILLING
knowing what we know NOW,
yes but at the time -

                    SMITH
was anybody in the office of
intelligence court
martialed after the Indy
sank?

Admiral Pilling realizes he is beyond
any hope of talking his way out of this
one, and he doesn't appear to like it

at all. His answers, which had been
carefully worded before, instead
become brief jabs.

                    PILLING
        No.

                    SMITH
        No. Well, was it an error in
        judgment for Commodore
        Gillette to turn those tugs
        around that first night?

                    PILLING
        Yes, of course.

                    SMITH
        Was Commodore Gillette
        court martialed for his
        glaring lack of judgment?

                    PILLING
        No.

                    SMITH
        No. It sure looks like
        there's enough error in
        judgment to go around. So
        was anybody else at all
        court martialed after the
        Indy sank?

                    PILLING
        No.

                    SMITH
          No.

Smith turns his attention away from
Pilling and directs his next
statements at the panel.

                    SMITH (CONT'D)
          If a law must be applied, it
          must be applied equally in
          order for it to be just.
          There is an inconsistency
          here. If you're going to use
          the principles of
          accountability, then you
          have to apply them to all
          officers who are involved.
          What I'm saying is if you're
          going to do this to one man,
          you've got to do it to EVERY
          man that was involved. That
          did not happen. That's why
          we're here. Not to rewrite
          history, but to make it
          fair.

Smith turns to address the gallery. He
gestures with his hands as he speaks.

                    SMITH (CONT'D)
Rear Admiral Hutson said
that the sinking of the USS
Indianapolis had nothing to
do with the court martial of
Captain McVay. Who here
believes that? Anybody?

The general perception of course, is
that it did.

Senator Smith turn's attention back
to Pilling, who looks none too happy
to be back in the hot seat.

                    SMITH (CONT'D)
Isn't it fair to say that
because Captain McVay was
court martialed, he looked
guilty as hell? Isn't that
why he got hate mail from the
families of the men who were
lost, right up until the day
he died?

Admiral Pilling struggles to maintain
the navy's position that one thing had
nothing to do with the other.

                    PILLING
Captain McVay was not court
martialed because the ship
sank.

                    SMITH
Gillette didn't get hate
mail every Christmas, did
he? Young didn't. Neither
did Seaman Alan, did he?
Birthdays, thanksgivings
and Rosh Hashanah came and
went for them without hate
mail.

                    PILLING
I wouldn't know.

                    SMITH
Of course you wouldn't.
Suppose all eleven hundred
and ninety-seven men came
into port alive, with the
ship in good shape. No five
days of shark attacks. No
exposure to weather and the
water. No fires. No
abandoned search. No
withholding of evidence.
None of the things that
happened. Just suppose
that. You're telling me the
captain would still have
been court martialed
because he didn't zig zag?

Admiral Pilling pauses, and senator
Smith advances upon him.

                    SMITH (CONT'D)
          Of course he wouldn't have.

                    ADMIRAL PILLING
          I don't know that.

                    SMITH
          Yes you do. And so does
          everyone here.

Smith waves his hand at the room,
where heads are nodding in agreement.

                    SMITH (CONT'D)
          Admiral Pilling, was the
          court martial of Captain
          Charles Butler McVay the
          third wrong?

Pilling sits, glaring at Smith.

Smith glares back.

                    SMITH (CONT'D)
          WAS IT WRONG?

ADMIRAL PILLING GIVES THE ANSWER HE CAN NO
LONGER AVOID.

                    PILLING
          Yes.

Senator Smith pauses, incredulous. He
was ready to keep fighting for the

truth, but there it was, right in
front of him.

Hunter gapes. He had hoped to hear it,
but didn't really believe that he
would.

The survivors react emotionally.
Finally, they have heard the truth
that they've been waiting for so long
to hear.

Senator Smith steps back from Admiral
Pilling, regarding him with a measure
of respect.

                    SMITH
          Thank you, Admiral Pilling.

Smith turns back to face the panel.

                    SMITH (CONT'D)
          That, gentlemen, is all we
          want. For the Navy to admit
          that Charles Butler McVay
          was a hell of an officer. He
          wouldn't have been given the
          bomb to take to the Enola Gay
          if he wasn't. We have a
          chance here, NOW to do the
          right thing. Finally. The
          truth is out now. All we ask
          is to make it right.

Senator Smith finishes. Chairman
Warner addresses Hunter.

                    CHAIRMAN WARNER
          Mr. Scott, do you have any
          further statements?

                    HUNTER
          Yes, Sir. Thank you. I carry
          this dog tag to remind me of
          the privilege and
          responsibility that I have
          to carry forward the torch
          of honor passed to me by the
          men of the USS Indianapolis.
          When I started this mission,
          there were a hundred and
          fifty-four survivors.
          Today, there are a hundred
          and thirty-four still with
          us. Please honor these men
          with the passage of Senate
          Resolution twenty-six.
          Please restore the honor of
          their ship, while some of
          these men are still alive to
          see the dream become a
          reality.

While Hunter speaks, the survivors in
attendance rise one by one, and stand
silently. Hunter pauses, turns and
looks at them with unashamed
admiration and turns back to face the
Senate.

Hunter stands with his heroes, and
holds up his fist, from which dangle
the dog tags of captain Charles Butler
McVay.

His tone both beseeches and dares the committee before which he's speaking.

                    HUNTER (CONT'D)
          Please. These men were
          forgotten once, when they
          were in the ocean. Do not
          forget the men of the USS
          Indianapolis for a second
          time

Hunter pauses for the most dramatic effect.

                    HUNTER (CONT'D)
          Please pass resolution 26.
          Thank you.

After a moment of contemplation, chairman Warner speaks.

                    WARNER
          I came into these
          proceedings with a
          determined frame of mind
          about them. Not a favorable
          one. However, hearing the
          new evidence, the
          testimony, and hearing the
          testimony of the survivors
          today, my perceptions have
          changed.

Warner looks at Hunter Scott.

WARNER (CONT'D)
To borrow a term from the
Navy, young man, you have
righted my course.

INT - HALLWAY OUTSIDE THE HEARING ROOM

Admiral Pilling is in the hallway,
dressing down a couple of his staff.
He's got to take it out on somebody.

PILLING
How the hell did you not know
about that report? How did
that kid come up with all
that information? What the
hell have you been doing?
Sitting on your hands?

At the same time, elsewhere in the
hallway, the survivors pose for a
group photograph, with Hunter Scott
and Senator Smith in the middle.

Hunter asks Senator Smith:

HUNTER
What do we do now?

SMITH
We wait. Don't worry.
They'll let us know how they
decide.

After the photo is taken, Hunter
notices Admiral Pilling's upset
demeanor toward his staff. Hunter
approaches Admiral Pilling.

                    HUNTER
          Excuse me, Sir. I'd like to
          give you a copy of my
          research. I think this will
          provide you with some of the
          answers you were looking
          for.

Admiral Pilling maintains his
military bearing, but stiffens
visibly. He takes the packet of
information that Hunter hands him and
struggles to answer politely.

                    PILLING
          Thank you.

Hunter leaves, and Pilling turns back
to his staff. The Admiral does not
look pleased at all.

                    PILLING (CONT'D)
          I am a career Admiral in the
          Navy. I have a Ph.D. from
          Cambridge. And I just got
          schooled by a fourteen year-
          old kid.

His staff nod. There will probably be
hell to pay for the gesture later, but

they can't help agreeing. He did get
schooled.

Hunter walks away from the scene
smiling. A very slight pump of his
fist at his side goes unnoticed by
all. Yes. He did school the Admiral,
and it felt good.

Hunter goes out the door to the
brilliant light of day.

EXT - A FISHING BOAT - DAY

Hunter and his father are in a boat on
a glistening body of water. They are
fishing.

The cell phone rings. Alan answers it.

                    ALAN
          Hello? Yes?

Alan holds out the phone to Hunter.

                    ALAN (CONT'D)
          It's for you, son.

Hunter takes the phone and puts it to
his ear.

                    HUNTER
          Hello?

There is a pause.

                    HUNTER (CONT'D)
          Mr. President?

Hunter listens for a moment.

                    HUNTER (CONT'D)
          Thank you, sir.

Hunter gives the phone back to his
father and smiles. Alan doesn't ask.
He's pretty sure what happened, and
when Hunter is ready, he will talk
about it.

                    HUNTER (CONT'D)
                 (VO)
          The men of the Indianapolis
          received a Presidential
          Unit Citation and a
          statement of no culpability
          was entered into Captain
          McVay's record. The court
          martial was not morally
          sustainable. It wasn't his
          fault. Resolution
          Twenty-six passed.

Hunter turns to look out across the
water. Before him, the water
stretches out from the bow of the boat
he's sitting in, to the distance.

                    DISSOLVE TO:

Dissolve from one body of water to
another. Pan up the vast bow of the

Indianapolis, intact. Her crew is
standing on the deck in formation.
They salute their captain.

Standing where he belongs, on the
command deck of his ship, Captain
McVay turns his face into the sun and
smiles.

                    TITLE OVER:

Today, Hunter Scott is thirty years
old. Carrying on in the tradition of
his heroes, he attended the Naval
Academy.

                    FADE TO:

Hunter as he looks today.

WHILE THE FINAL CREDITS RUN:

One by one, we see pictures of the men
who served aboard the USS
Indianapolis. We see the man who
survived, and the ones who perished.
All of them.

FADE TO BLACK

Hunter Scott wrote a book about his involvement with the USS Indianapolis and her crew.

It's called Left For Dead, and can be found wherever books are sold.

Jeannie Depp continues to write screenplays, books and graphic novels. She is also an artist living outside Baton Rouge.

www.ingramcontent.com/pod-product-compliance
Lightning Source LLC
Chambersburg PA
CBHW070632030426
42337CB00020B/3991